D0319927

Illingworth's War in Cartoons

Also by Mark Bryant

Dictionary of British Cartoonists and Caricaturists, 1730-1980 (with S. Heneage)

Dictionary of Twentieth-Century British Cartoonists and Caricaturists

Napoleonic Wars in Cartoons

Wars of Empire in Cartoons

World War I in Cartoons

World War II in Cartoons

God in Cartoons

The Complete Colonel Blimp (ed.)

The Comic Cruikshank (ed.)

Vicky's Supermac (ed.)

H.M.Bateman (ed.)

Nicolas Bentley (ed.)

Illingworth's War in Cartoons

One Hundred of His Greatest Drawings from the *Daily Mail*, 1939-1945

Mark Bryant

Grub Street • London

For Pamela and Francis Wilford-Smith

First published 2009 by
Grub Street Publishing
4 Rainham Close
London SW11 6SS

Copyright © Mark Bryant 2009
Cartoons copyright
© Solo Syndication/Associated Newspapers

British Library Cataloguing in Publication Data
Bryant, Mark, 1953-
Illingworth's war in cartoons: one hundred of his
greatest drawings 1939-1945.
   1. Illingworth, Leslie Gilbert, 1902-1979.
   2. World War, 1939-1945 – Caricatures andcartoons.
   3. Cartoonists – Great Britain – Biography.
   I. Title II. National Library of Wales. III. Daily Mail.
   940.5'3'0222-dc22

ISBN-13: 9781906502546

The moral right of the author has been asserted.

All rights reserved. No part of this publication may be
reproduced, stored in a retrieval system, or transmitted
in any form or by any means electronic, mechanical,
photocopying, recording, or otherwise, without the prior
permission of the copyright owner.

Designed by Roy Platten, Eclipse.
roy.eclipse@btopenworld.com

Printed by the MPG Books Group, Bodmin & King's Lynn
on FSC approved paper

Page 1:   *Daily Mail*, 24 December 1940
Page 3:   **Flag Day in Munich**, *Daily Mail*, 19 June 1940
Page 4:   **The End in Sight**, *Daily Mail*, 23 August 1944
Page 5:   **Well, Orders are Orders**, *Daily Mail*,
             22 November 1941
Page 6:   **Running Out**, *Daily Mail*, 28 September 1942
Page 9:   Composite Illingworth drawing
             (created by Mark Bryant 2002)

Contents

Foreword

THE FINEST CARTOONISTS OF the Second World War were David Low of the *Evening Standard*, famous for Colonel Blimp; Fougasse for his posters such as 'Careless Talk Costs Lives'; Zec at the *Daily Mirror* for 'The Price of Petrol' – the cartoon that offended Churchill; and Illingworth of the *Daily Mail*. But it is Illingworth who has most slipped out of our collective memory and that is clearly unjust. One of the reasons for this is that very few of his cartoons come up at auction; indeed there are not many Illingworth collectors which is not surprising when 5,000 of his cartoons are stored at the National Library of Wales in Aberystwyth. Aberystwyth because Illingworth started his life in Wales, although his main cartooning years were spent in Northcliffe House in Fleet Street, London.

Illingworth applied for the post of cartoonist in 1939 and throughout the war he produced four cartoons a week for the *Daily Mail* and occasionally some for *Punch*: that was a demanding schedule. His cartoons became so well-known that the Nazis put his name on the Gestapo death-list. The actual cartoons are very finely drawn – they are the work essentially of an illustrator: precise, careful and meticulous for, after all, he had earned his living as an illustrator in the 1930s.

One of his great advantages was that he had actually seen Hitler and Goering in person which made his drawings more vivid and accurate. Hitler is shown as an over-active maniac and Goering as a relentless juggernaut. The Nazis were generally depicted in his cartoons as a bunch of slaughtering tyrants, often in the guise of Death. One of the most chilling was in 1941 when the figure of Justice, dressed in a Nazi uniform, weighs the balance between Nazi oppression and the execution by firing squad of fifty French citizens as a reprisal for the murder of Lieutenant-Colonel Holz, the German Commandant of Nantes.

There are many other memorable images: after the fall of France in July 1940 Hitler advances as a dentist upon John Bull, the last, awkward, aching tooth, but he will never be pulled out; Napoleon's ghost on the shore at Calais saying, 'That's as far as *I* got, Adolf'; and after the Battle of Stalingrad Stalin is a great porcupine resisting Hitler's German Shepherd.

These patriotic cartoons remind you of their powerful impact when our country was fighting for its life. There are no shades of grey: black and white are the colours, and black and white is the choice between good and evil. The Nazis were evil and had to be stopped and that can be portrayed more vividly in a drawing than five column inches of print. There is no doubt that Illingworth's constant reminder of the threat facing us in 1939-45 helped to galvanise the national spirit of the British people. We should all be grateful to Mark Bryant as the pioneer in bringing the work of Leslie Illingworth to a wider audience.

Kenneth Baker

Lord Baker of Dorking

Preface

THIS BOOK HAS BEEN PUBLISHED TO commemorate the thirtieth anniversary of the death of the political cartoonist Leslie Illingworth as well as the seventieth anniversary of his joining the *Daily Mail* at the beginning of the Second World War.

Despite being one of the twentieth century's greatest graphic artists and illustrators, very little has been recorded or published about his life, works and attitudes. In 1996 I came across a large uncatalogued deposit of some 5000 of his original *Daily Mail* political cartoons in the archives of the National Library of Wales in Aberystwyth. This became the basis for my PhD on the role of the political cartoonist in wartime, stretching back to Gillray and the Napoleonic Wars but focussing in particular on Illingworth and the Second World War. In the course of my research for this – as well as for my essays on Illingworth for the *Oxford Dictionary of National Biography* and the *Journal of European Studies* – my knowledge of the artist grew and eventually resulted in the first major exhibition of his original wartime cartoons from the *Daily Mail* which I curated for the National Library of Wales in 2005.

Like the exhibition itself, the task of selecting which cartoons to include in this modest anthology of his wartime drawings has not been easy. In all, Illingworth drew more than 1000 cartoons for the *Daily Mail* during the Second World War from 30 October 1939, when he began at the paper, until September 1945 when the war finally ended. In addition he drew about 100 cartoons for *Punch* during this period as well as a number for the Ministry of Information and other government departments.

In the end it was decided to include only those drawings for which originals exist at the National Library of Wales itself and to use the original artwork, even if there are small variations to the cartoons as published in the *Daily Mail*. The result is that Illingworth's drawings will be seen for the first time as they really were, unsullied by muddy wartime printing methods and poor-quality paper.

All those cartoons selected for the Aberystwyth exhibition have been included, as well as around 50 extra drawings from the collection of the National Library of Wales to make more than 100 altogether. Inevitably, there are gaps in the sequence where significant cartoons have been sold or have gone astray, and due to limitations of space no attempt has been made to give a comprehensive survey of the war years in his cartoons. Instead, a personal selection has been made of what I feel are some of Illingworth's most powerful and dramatic surviving *Daily Mail* drawings from the Second World War. Also, as 70 years have now passed since their first publication, some brief historical notes have been added to put them in context.

In preparing this book, as well as the earlier exhibition and publications, I have been immensely indebted to a number of people and institutions and would like to acknowledge them here. Many thanks, first of all, go to Richard Illingworth and the family of Leslie Illingworth. Also to Illingworth's close friends: Francis Wilford-Smith (the cartoonist Smilby) and his wife Pamela; Wally Fawkes (the cartoonist Trog) and his wife Sue; the American cartoonist and art historian Draper Hill (whose 1970 exhibition catalogue, *Illingworth on Target*, and other information were very useful); and cartoonists John Jensen and the late Clive Uptton.

Others who have been of help have included Geoffrey Beare, Rosemary Bragg, Jancie Brown, the late Sid Brown, Tom Curtis, Jane Davies, Charlotte Fairlie, Michael Foot, Neil Fowler, Colette Fyfe, Nicholas Garland, Dr Dennis Griffiths, Phil Hall, the late Harry Hargreaves, the late Bill Hewison, Dr Valerie Holman, the late Peter Jackson, Tegwyn Jones, David Langdon, the late Terence Parkes ('Larry'), Julian Lewis, MAC (Stan McMurtry), Ken Mahood, Peter Mellini, Ursula Niebour, Emma O'Grady, Per Marquard Otzen, Gavin Perkins, Sylvia Philpin Jones, the late Jeremy Phipps, Bryan Reading, Ralph and Anna Steadman, Kevin Swan, Keith Waite, Sian and Julian Walford, and Diana and Richard Willis.

I would also like to thank the staff of the various institutions in whose archives and libraries I have worked, or with whom I have corresponded. Foremost amongst these are the Cartoon Museum, British Cartoonists' Association, British Library, British Museum Department of Prints & Drawings, British Newspaper Library, *Daily Mail* Reference Library, Cardiff Public Library, Imperial War Museum Library and Department of Art, John Frost Newspapers, Karikatur & Cartoon Museum Basel, London Library, London Press Club, National Library of Wales (Aberystwyth), National Portrait Gallery, Public Records Office, *Punch* Library, Rae-Smith Gallery, St Bride Printing Library, Tate Gallery, University of London Senate House Library, Victoria & Albert Museum Library, *Western Mail* Library & Archives (Cardiff), and the Westminster Central Reference Library.

A particular debt of honour must also go to the late Keith Mackenzie who was a close friend of Illingworth and whose notes and tape-recorded interviews (as well as those by Francis Wilford-Smith and others) have been of considerable help. Also to my late father, Bob Bryant, whose collection of wartime cartoon books bought while he was serving in the RAF in Burma in the Second World War, formed some of my earliest cartoon memories.

Special thanks are also due to Professors David Welch and Colin Seymour-Ure of the University of Kent for their guidance and support while studying for my PhD, and to Dr Nicholas Hiley, Jane Newton and all the staff at the British Cartoon Archive at the University of Kent, custodians of the Illingworth Papers. I am also extremely grateful to Dr Michael Francis, Dr Huw Owen and the staff of the National Library of Wales, Aberystwyth, especially Arwel Jones and Jamie Thomas; to Robin Esser, Paul Rossiter and Steve Torrington of the *Daily Mail*; and Bill Gardiner and Danny Howell of Solo Syndication. I am also greatly indebted to Lord Baker of Dorking, Patron of the Cartoon Museum, for his splendid Foreword. Last, but by no means least, many thanks go to John Davies, Anne Dolamore and Hannah Stuart of Grub Street – and the designer Roy Platten – for producing such an attractive volume.

Mark Bryant
London

Leslie Illingworth in his wartime studio at the *Daily Mail*. The photo is undated but as the cartoon he is working on is 'Here He Comes!' (15 May 1944) featuring a cricket match with Eisenhower as the bowler, Hitler as the batsman and Stalin as the wicket-keeper, it was probably taken either that day (a Monday) or, more likely, the day before. (*Photo courtesy of the British Cartoon Archive, University of Kent. Crown copyright, reproduced with permission.*)

Introduction

ON 4 NOVEMBER 1899, at the beginning of the Boer War and only three years after the *Daily Mail* was founded, an editorial declared: 'Now that the war has begun in grim earnest there is a chance for some ambitious cartoonist to make a great reputation. A political cartoonist is the rarest of all artists.' No one of sufficient stature arose to work for the newspaper then, nor through the many international conflicts which followed. However, almost exactly forty years later, on 30 October 1939 at the beginning of the Second World War, Leslie Illingworth was taken on by the *Daily Mail* as its first ever staff political cartoonist in wartime.

In many ways it can be argued that during the Second World War the daily newspaper political cartoon reached the peak of its achievement, both technically and with regard to its power and impact (via the mass media) on a wide public. Though the history of graphic satire in wartime can be traced back centuries in Britain – to James Gillray and the Napoleonic Wars and to the artists of the weekly *Punch* (founded in 1841 during the First Afghan War) – there are a number of reasons for holding this view.

Offset lithographic printing using rotary presses (only introduced in the 1890s) had by the late 1930s reached full development, allowing for the first time the mass production of illustrations, including cartoons, on cheap newsprint paper. This would be of especial importance when high quality wood pulp became scarce after the Nazi occupation of Scandinavia and U-boat blockades limited its subsequent importation from Canada.

Photographs, in contrast to cartoons, were frequently censored during the war, required better quality paper than drawings and were less immediate (they often took days to arrive from the Front Line and air mail was very limited). Also, as mere records of events, they told less of a story than cartoons.

In addition, in the 1930s, cartoons (whether in monochrome in newspapers or in colour on posters) were a significant form of pictorial information – television was then in its infancy and newsreels were often out of date by the time they reached the cinemas. Though radio and the printed word were the prime methods of communication, cartoons gave the public not only news, propaganda and assurance but also graphic images of the leading political figures of the day, at home and abroad – especially as caricatures of individuals increasingly began to replace the old national symbols such as Britannia, John Bull and the British Lion.

By having few or no words, a cartoon can also communicate quickly and powerfully to everyone. As Adolf Hitler said in *Mein Kampf* (1925): 'At one stroke... people will understand a pictorial presentation of something which it would take them a long and laborious effort of reading to understand.' This was an essential attribute in wartime, but especially during the Second World War when it was necessary to communicate not only with many foreign allies overseas but also with the thousands of foreigners either stationed in Britain as troops or living in the country as exiles, many of whom could not read English well.

In addition, as some newspapers were (at the beginning of the war) widely distributed internationally, there was also the propaganda value of the pictures when they were seen by readers in enemy countries – Germans, Italians etc. – whether or not they spoke English. Anyone who could recognise Hitler or Mussolini from photos, films or portraits could recognise them transformed into grotesque animals or monsters – so long as the drawing quality was good enough in each case.

The Second World War, far more than the Great War, was also the first 'total war', involving civilians at home as well as military forces, and hence the cartoonist's subject matter was broader than ever before, from air-raid shelters and the blackout to food rationing and the Home Guard. It was also something about which the general public had an insatiable appetite for information. As Thomas Hardy said in *The Dynasts* (1904) – his play about the Napoleonic Wars – 'War makes rattling good history; but Peace is poor reading.'

Finally, the fast-growing markets for cartoons generally at this time (in magazines, newspapers, advertising etc.) led to the appearance of a large number of extremely gifted full- and part-time cartoonists – encouraged by correspondence courses in art – and so competition became intense and standards rose even higher.

However, this power of the political newspaper cartoon in Britain as a visual information and propaganda medium did not last long. Magazines like *Picture Post*, launched in 1938 by Stefan Lorant (the editor of *Lilliput*), led the way in photo-journalism and daily newspapers followed soon afterwards. Since the 1950s, with the widespread availability of television, and more recently with the advent of the Internet, the role of the daily newspaper itself – and hence of the daily political cartoon – has decreased considerably.

In looking at the Second World War, many British history books – if they use cartoons at all – tend to concentrate on the artists of the weekly *Punch* and the work of David Low of the London *Evening Standard*, many of whose drawings have been preserved in books and anthologies. As a result, a great many other distinguished wartime cartoonists have often been overlooked. Like the works of their fellow print journalists their daily creative efforts were usually consigned to the waste-bin at sundown or used to wrap fish and chips, line drawers or light fires. If their drawings survived at all they can now only be seen in press archives, newspaper libraries or, very occasionally, as originals in museums, libraries and art galleries.

Added to which, concentration on these two publications gives a misleading view of the cartoon scene in Britain in the 1930s and 40s. Not only were there a number of other important artists working as political cartoonists for major national daily and weekly newspapers at the time – such as Strube, Zec, Whitelaw, Gabriel, Vicky, Stephen, Giles, Bert Thomas and Clive Uptton – but their drawings would also have been seen by literally millions of readers.

Even though the *Daily Mail* was only the fourth largest newspaper in Britain during the war years (after the *Express*, *Herald* and *Mirror*), it nonetheless sold nearly 1,600,000 copies nationwide every day, six days a week (not including the international edition) – four times as many as *Punch* and the *Evening Standard* combined.[1] As the historian Dr Adrian Smith noted in an article in *Encounter* in 1985, despite Low's work being widely syndicated: 'The vast majority of newspaper readers in the late 1930s...never saw Low's drawings on a regular basis.' The same held true of the wartime political cartoons of Sir Bernard Parridge, E.H.Shepard and others on the weekly *Punch*.

In addition, though Low (who was later knighted for his work) was undeniably a great artist – perhaps one of the greatest political cartoonists of the twentieth century – he was, in many ways, not a typical wartime daily newspaper cartoonist. Not only did he draw for a small-circulation London (not national) evening paper, whose sales were even outstripped by its wartime rivals the *Star* and the *Evening News*, but also he was not a staff artist but rather a 'signed contributor'. Added to which, he did not even work in Fleet Street – his single daily drawing being collected by messenger from his studio five miles away in the north London suburb of Hampstead and delivered to the *Evening Standard*'s City offices in Shoe Lane.

By contrast Leslie Illingworth of the *Daily Mail* was a staff member of a large-circulation national morning paper read regularly by a significant part of the British public and, via its international edition, worldwide. He also worked in the newspaper's offices in Northcliffe House, located just off Fleet Street and near St Paul's at the centre of the London Blitz.

Yet despite all this, Illingworth's name is not well-known today. This was not always the case, particularly during the war years. Low had worked for the *Evening Standard* since 1927 yet by 1944 – only five years after Illingworth joined the *Daily Mail* – an article in the US magazine *Newsweek* declared that 'nearly all agree he is Low's

---

1 The top-selling title in 1939 was the *Daily Express* (2,546,000), followed by the *Daily Herald* (1,850,000) and the *Daily Mirror* (1,571,000). The circulation of the London *Evening Standard* (382,000) was only three times that of the weekly magazine *Punch* (116,000).

outstanding rival' and, in some critics' eyes at least, he had the edge. In his obituary of Illingworth for the *Guardian* (22 December 1979) Malcolm Muggeridge, a former editor of *Punch*, wrote:

> I think myself that a collection of his best cartoons will, in the long run, wear better than one of David Low's: the reason being that Low's cartoons usually relate to some immediate situation which soon gets forgotten, whereas Illingworth's go deeper, becoming, at their best, satire in the grand style rather than mischievous quips; strategic rather than practical.

Hence this long-overdue collection of Illingworth's wartime drawings from the *Daily Mail*. It is to be hoped that, though only a relatively slim volume, it will go some way to redressing the balance of British political cartoons of the Second World War and at the same time may help revive the reputation of one of the twentieth-century's greatest graphic artists. As Keith Mackenzie (Art Editor of Associated Newspapers) said in *The Artist* in 1969:

> Leslie Gilbert Illingworth could be described as the last of the great penmen in the line of English social satirists starting with Hogarth and traceable through the biting and rumbustious broadsides of Rowlandson, Gillray and Cruikshank to the more moderate social comments of Leech, Tenniel, Keene and Phil May...it is fairly safe to assume that when the history of cartoon and caricature comes to be written the name of Illingworth will have a valued place in the tradition of great political satire of this century, along with Will Dyson, Low, Giles, Vicky and Osbert Lancaster.

Illingworth's Early Beginnings as a Cartoonist

Leslie Gilbert Illingworth was born on 2 September 1902 at 9 Harbour Road, in the respectable 'executive part' of the port of Barry, near Cardiff. He was the second son of Richard ('Dick') Frederick Illingworth (1866-1956), from Knutsford, Cheshire, but of a Yorkshire family, who moved to Wales in 1890 to become a clerk (later chief clerk) in the engineers' department of the newly founded Barry Railway & Docks Company. His mother, Helen MacGregor (1874-1952), a teacher, was born in Hull of Scottish parents.

Leslie's elder brother, Lieutenant-Colonel Vivian Richard Illingworth OBE (1899-1944), was a successful civil engineer working for Great Western Railways. Though exempted as a railway employee, Vivian had volunteered for the army in the First World War (achieving a commission in 1919) and had then joined the Army Supplementary Reserve in peacetime. Despite his age at the outbreak of the Second World War he served as a railway construction engineer and quickly attained high rank (and was mentioned in dispatches). He died of leukaemia while on active duty in Naples on 2 February 1944. Leslie also had a younger sister, Phyllis Jean Illingworth (later Lewis, 1905-97) who graduated from Homerton College, Cambridge University, and became a teacher in Wales.

The family moved to No.1 Cardiff Road, a large house with stables situated close to the railway station, in the village of Cadoxton, near Barry, in about 1904 and Illingworth was educated at Palmerston Road Infants School there. It was in Cadoxton that he began drawing, at the age of four, in the forge of the village blacksmith Evan Hopkins (known familiarly as 'Ianto the Forge'). As Illingworth later recalled: 'He started me off as a caricaturist, for the first public drawing I ever did was of Tom Llewelyn, Glebe Farm, with his arm in a sling. I did it on the tarred door of the forge with a lump of chalk which Ianto gave me.'

In about 1912 the family moved again, to Gileston. Here he went to St Athan School, run by Jack Thomas ('Thomas the School') and was encouraged in his art by Rev. George Jenkins, the Rector of St Athan, and his wife, who allowed him to copy cartoons from their collection of bound volumes of *Punch* (Illingworth later owned two original Charles Keene drawings). He was also impressed by paintings by Lely and others – as well as prints by Rackham and Dulac – that hung in the rectory, and like his father became a great admirer of the magazine illustrator Frank Craig (1874-1918), some of whose paintings hung in County Hall, Cardiff.

In later life Illingworth would claim that he always wanted to be a cartoonist and that his interest dated from this period. For him art was, as he often said, an 'instead of' – it was something you did when you were unable to do anything else. He felt he had not been very bright academically, was not particularly good at sport or music, and had no talent for business, so drawing was what he concentrated on. He was also not a great wordsmith or public speaker, later confessing: 'I hate to speak in public. I am not at ease with words. I forget the names and I am a man who thinks with pictures not words.' So to be an artist was the ideal solution.

One of his uncles was Frank William Illingworth (1888-1972), a primary school teacher in Wallasey who had himself taken evening art classes and had studied by correspondence course with Percy V. Bradshaw's Press Art School in London. He had also had a drawing published in *Punch* – the famous First World War cartoon 'Do I know if the Rooshuns has really come through England?' (*Punch*, 23 September 1914).[2] Though Uncle Frank lived in Nantwich, Cheshire, he often visited the Glamorgan Illingworths and it was probably on one of these visits that he lent his Press Art School course notes to the young Leslie. That the boy studied these (and hence indirectly became another pupil of Bradshaw, whose alumni included the famous cartoonists Fougasse, Leo Cheney, Norman Pett and Joe Lee) was confirmed in Bradshaw's wartime interview with him for *London Opinion* (December 1941).

This period also saw the growth of Illingworth's other great love, farming, and he often liked to visit neighbouring farms and watch the farmworkers and livestock.[3] He later said that if he had not become a cartoonist he'd have liked to have been an animal painter like Landseer or an animal illustrator like Warwick Reynolds. It is a tribute to his love of the countryside and his skills in draughtsmanship that Sir Alfred Munnings (a former president of the Royal Academy) later praised one of his *Daily Mail* drawings which featured a cornfield ('It Won't Be Long Now', 20 September 1951): 'Illingworth in his cartoon today has surpassed himself. Not only is it correct in every detail, agricultural and otherwise, but he has reached the heights of cartooning and merriment. In fact it is the funniest thing in years.'

When he left St Athan School Illingworth won a scholarship to Barry County Boys' (Grammar) School under headmaster Major Edgar Jones. Here a fellow pupil and close friend was Ronald Niebour, who was also later to become a cartoonist, first in Barry and later, under the pseudonym 'Neb', with the *Daily Mail* (joining the year before Illingworth).[4] Then, at the age of 15, Illingworth won another scholarship, to study art under Wilson Jagger at Cardiff Art School (then known as the City of Cardiff Technical College & Art School), whose former pupils had included the sculptor Sir William Goscombe John RA. Here he won a gold medal for drawing and had four topical cartoons published in the college's magazine, *Pen and Pencil*, in April 1920.

For three years (1917-20) Illingworth studied at college in the mornings (until noon) and evenings. In the afternoons, for nine months, he worked in the lithographic department of the Cardiff-based *Western Mail* – the main daily newspaper of Wales – designing rolls of honour for First World War troops, producing illuminated addresses, taking on various commercial printing jobs and later also producing police court drawings.[5]

It was at the *Western Mail*'s premises that he produced his first paid humorous drawing (a design for a railway timetable cover). This led to his being commissioned to take over the regular football cartoon ('Dai Pepper') on the *Football Express*, the Saturday supplement of the *Western Mail*'s sister title the *Evening Express*. 'Dai Pepper' had originally been drawn by J.M.Staniforth ('JMS', 1863-1921), the distinguished and long-serving political cartoonist on the *Western Mail* – and one of Britain's first war cartoonists on a daily newspaper (albeit a regional one) – and Illingworth was encouraged and given some tips by him.

Illingworth also became friendly with Dai John (1884-1958), the sports cartoonist of the *Football Echo* (part of the *South Wales Echo*, a rival to the *Evening Express*) and creator of the character 'Dai Lossin'. Illingworth was a great admirer of his work, especially as John had lost the use of his right arm during the First World War.

It is highly probable that Illingworth was by then also aware of the great Welsh cartoonists of the past such as the early *Punch* artist Kenny Meadows (1790-1874) and his own near contemporaries Quiz (Powys Evans, 1899-1981)

---

2   According to his daughter Rosemary Bragg this was the only cartoon he ever had published.

3   The political cartoonist Trog (Wally Fawkes, b.1924) – who was greatly influenced by Illingworth and later succeeded him at the *Daily Mail* – even depicted him as the Welsh farmer character 'Organ Morgan' in his satirical strip 'Flook' in the 1970s. Such was the attraction of the countryside that Illingworth later became a farmer himself. Having kept goats in his house in Povey Cross (c.1940-46) he then bought a 12-acre smallholding, 'Silverdale' in Robertsbridge, Sussex, and kept three cows, many cats and a poodle.

4   At the end of the war British Foundation Pictures Ltd, in conjunction with the *Daily Mail*, made a two-reel feature film, *The Birth of a Notion* (1945) featuring Illingworth and Neb. The commentary was by the BBC's Frank Phillips and there were location shots of South Wales, birthplace of both artists.

5   According to a handwritten document by Robert (later Sir Robert) Webber (managing director of the *Western Mail*) in the *Western Mail*'s archives (dated 19 November 1940) it was Webber himself who first became aware of Illingworth's work while he was still at school, invited him to become an apprentice in the *Western Mail*'s art department under W.H.J.Richard, and advised him to take art classes at Cardiff Art School.

and the famous Great War cartoonist Bert Thomas MBE (1883-1966), celebrated for his ' 'Arf a Mo', Kaiser' drawing and for producing Britain's largest poster (for the War Bonds campaign) which was 75 feet long and covered the face of the National Gallery in London (Thomas was also later Illingworth's opposite number on the *Daily Mail*'s sister paper the *Evening News* during the Second World War and produced the best known version of the poster 'Is Your Journey Really Necessary?' – see page 89).

In 1921 Illingworth won a three-year scholarship (worth £90 a year) to study in London under Sir William Rothenstein at the Royal College of Art, then based in Exhibition Road, South Kensington. This period at the RCA was a particularly fruitful one and famous contemporaries included Barbara Hepworth, Henry Moore, Eric Ravilious, Edward Bawden, Raymond Coxon, A.K.Lawrence and the bird painter Charles Tunnicliffe. Another fellow student was John Gilroy, later to become famous for his advertising cartoons, notably the Guinness series, and during the Second World War for his Ministry of Information posters (e.g. 'Make Do and Mend' and 'Keep it Under Your Hat'). In addition, one of Illingworth's teachers at the RCA was the illustrator, painter and cartoonist Thomas Derrick ARCA who had been art advisor to the government's Foreign Propaganda Department during the First World War.

Though by this time living in London at 3 Battersea Bridge Road West, Illingworth continued to draw his weekly cartoons for the *Football Express*. Then when the 58-year-old Staniforth became ill, Illingworth's father – who played golf with the *Western Mail*'s managing director Robert J. Webber (Dick Illingworth was a founder member and later secretary of the club) – suggested that his son should be Staniforth's understudy. His first political cartoon appeared in the paper on Tuesday 11 October 1921, signed 'L.G.Illingworth'.[6]

From the *Western Mail* to the *Daily Mail*

J.M. Staniforth died on 17 December 1921, earning personal tributes from the Welsh-born Prime Minister Lloyd George (prime minister from 1916 to 1922) amongst other celebrities. As a result, Illingworth took over his job and began to work on the paper (three months after his 19th birthday), then edited by Sir William Davies, for £6 a week.

For a while Illingworth continued to study and live in London but by the time he was 20 he was earning the then high sum of £1000 a year from the *Western Mail* and other work (his father, who had a senior and responsible job in charge of 300 clerks, had only been earning c. £360 p.a. in 1920). As a result he decided to give up his studies at the RCA and returned to Wales to live with his parents and sister in Gileston, cycling into Cardiff each day.

He eventually drew one political cartoon plus a children's feature ('Aunt Betty's' cartoon) each day for the paper as well as a weekly cartoon for the Saturday *Weekly Mail* and sundry illustrations. In addition, between March 1922 (when it was launched) and February 1924 he drew 21 caricatures of musical personalities for the Welsh-language monthly music magazine *Y Cerddor Newydd* (The New Musician) published by Hughes & Son of Wrexham and in 1922-23 illustrated at least three books published by the same company.

At about this time he also became friendly with the three Cardiff-born Cudlipp brothers, Percy (who became editor of the *Daily Herald* in 1940), Reginald (who was a sub-editor on the *Western Mail* and later became editor of the *News of the World*) and Hugh (the future editor of the *Sunday Pictorial*, later retitled the *Sunday Mirror*).

In November 1923, while Illingworth was still at the *Western Mail*, Owen Aves, himself a cartoonist and at that time art editor of the humorous weekly *The Passing Show*, sent him a joke featuring pigs to illustrate and subsequently invited him to submit work by post. Then when Aves left the magazine and set up as an artists' agent in June 1924 he took on Illingworth. This would lead to work for the *Humorist, London Opinion, Pearson's, Strand, Nash's, Good Housekeeping, London Life, Red Magazine, Wills' Magazine, Answers, Tit-Bits, Everybody's* and others.

Later in 1924 Illingworth moved to London to study (briefly) part-time at the Slade School of Art, London University, under Henry Tonks (who had been an official war artist in the First World War) while still drawing for the *Western Mail* and producing freelance work for Aves. However, in 1925 he returned to live in Wales when the family

6 In fact it was a joke about the weather: *'Jove (catching the Clerk of the Weather asleep at his post):* "May I drink the Styx if I don't get a new clerk; that's the second time this year he has left the hot weather tap running."'

moved about two miles from Gileston to the more spacious Picketston Cottage, near Picketston House (and farm), outside St Athan, working from a studio above the garage in a converted barn.

During the General Strike of 1926 the right-wing *Western Mail* took an uncompromising editorial stance attacking the miners – especially their leader A.J.Cook, who coined the phrase 'Not a minute on the day, not a penny off the pay'. Nonetheless Illingworth continued to work for the newspaper, producing his own plates when the print department refused to make them. Though his father was a stout Conservative, Illingworth was then himself a Socialist (he had read Marx and Engels) and felt uncomfortable with his situation. He later admitted 'I was a blackleg' but added: 'Nobody suggested ideas when I started in the *Western Mail*; I knew very well what the politics of the paper were, and I knew which side of my bread was buttered. The cartoonist must have a pragmatic approach.' (A favourite phrase of his was 'I am very venal' – he did it for the money.)

In an interview fifty years later Illingworth said that it was at about this time that he changed his political views, arguing that 'once you get into the romantic sort of politics you always start killing in the end, and it's bad, bad. I am against that', adding that: 'I sincerely believe we are all brothers and anybody who tries to put people against each other – that's cartoonists too – is doing the wrong thing.' Another phrase of which Illingworth was fond throughout his life was: 'I'm not a zealot in any way at all.' He once even went so far as to say of another political cartoonist: 'He's sincere. He's zealous, yes. And that's why he's an utter clot.'

In 1926 Illingworth took a sabbatical. According to Sir Robert Webber 'he was given a cheque and six months' leave of absence to tour the art schools of France and America, finally leaving Salt Lake City to resume his cartoons with the *Western Mail*'.

At the end of the following year he resigned. His last cartoon – 'Poor Old Father Christmas!', featuring Winston Churchill (who was chancellor of the exchequer, 1924-9) stealing 'Our Money' from Santa's sack – was published on Saturday 24 December 1927. According to his former schoolfriend and neighbour Harold Wrightson' he had become ill from overwork and threw in the job after returning from a holiday in Grindelwald, Switzerland. However, he had by then also built up a sizeable contacts list for freelance magazine illustration work and it is likely that his 'venal' streak may have had additional influence on his decision (prices for illustrations being twice those of the

Self-portraits of Leslie Illingworth, 1921-44
A shy man, Illingworth also had a very low opinion of his appearance and never thought himself attractive, as these three self-portraits show. He was of medium height, with a stocky build, a very large head and an undershot jaw. In his youth he had bright red hair which later turned white and increasingly large bushy eyebrows spread above his blue eyes. The first of these drawings (reproduced courtesy of Draper Hill) is from a student sketchbook dated 1921 (when he was 19), the second is from the 1930s and the third is from 1944.

Western Mail). This was confirmed by Webber who said: 'Eventually he asked to be released in order to take up illustrative work and in this branch of art he soon was amongst the top flight of British artists.'

After leaving the *Western Mail* Illingworth moved to Paris – where the devalued franc meant that living was cheap – to continue his art studies. However, not having the required baccalaureate in French for admission to the Ecole des Beaux-Arts, he took classes at the Académie Julian (where his former RCA head William Rothenstein had studied). While there he continued to produce freelance illustrations, cartoons and advertising work arranged by Aves and dispatched to London by air (there were at this time in Britain some 16 or more magazines which regularly commissioned story illustration work from freelancers).

In 1928 he accepted an invitation to stay with the political cartoonist Dorman H. Smith (of the NEA syndication agency), in Maplewood, New Jersey, USA. Taking his sister Phyllis with him he worked for three months as a political cartoonist for Hearst newspapers in New York (Hearst owned the British magazines *Good Housekeeping* and *Nash's* to which Illingworth had been a regular contributor) and also drew for *Life* and other publications. He then bought a car and drove with his sister to the West Coast.

Returning to Britain he moved to St John's Wood, London, to study briefly again at the Slade (1928-9) under Henry Tonks before returning to his parents' house in Picketston. Here he began freelancing once more, producing advertisements for the 'Beer is Best' campaign and for such clients as Winsor & Newton, Kraft Cheese, Grey's Cigarettes, Symingtons Soups, Eiffel Tower Lemonade and Wolsey Underwear and drawing illustrations for short stories in magazines such as the *Strand* for 75 guineas a time. By 1937 *The Artist* would describe him as 'among the half-dozen most eminent magazine artists of our day'.

At about this time he also began to draw cartoons for *Punch*, then edited by Sir Owen Seaman with the cartoonist George Morrow as art editor. However, his claim that his first work for the magazine was in 1927 seems to be mistaken as his own description of this first cartoon (an illustration for someone else's joke about a boy bursting a balloon-seller's balloons) exactly fits the magazine's first indexed entry for a cartoon under his name which was published on 27 May 1931.

Illingworth produced four more non-political cartoons for the magazine in 1931, three of which were full-page drawings. His first 'big cut', or whole-page political cartoon, for *Punch* ('The Line of Least Resistance' featuring F.D.Roosevelt) was published on 21 April 1937 during the editorship of E.V.Knox. He went on to draw seven more full-page political cartoons in 1937, six in 1938 and 11 in 1939, and then began alternating as second cartoonist with E.H.Shepard (of 'Winnie the Pooh' fame) when the main cartoonist, Sir Bernard Partridge (by then nearly 80), stopped coming to London with the outbreak of war. When Partridge died in 1945, Illingworth, who was seen as a better political cartoonist than Shepard, took over the main cartoon altogether. So successful was his work for the magazine that R.G.G.Price in his *A History of Punch* (1957) said: 'Illingworth was a superb draughtsman in a job that needed one.' Michael Cummings OBE (1919-97), political cartoonist of the *Daily Express*, later went further and declared that he was 'probably the most outstanding cartoonist that *Punch* ever had, better than Tenniel [...] and certainly better than Partridge'.

In 1936, aged 34, Illingworth finally left home and moved to London (the move coincided with the building of an RAF aerodrome next door to the Picketston house which may have hastened his departure). He answered an advertisement in *The Times* for a first-floor flat to let at 53 Queensborough Terrace, Bayswater, and it was here that he met his lifetime companion Enid Ratcliff, who leased him the apartment (No.5) for 37s.6d. a week.[7]

The Second World War broke out the day after Illingworth's 37th birthday. Though 40, his elder brother – an army reservist – joined up immediately but Illingworth himself was less sure of his future role. With the magazine market beginning to dry up because of wartime restrictions it is possible that he considered enlisting as an official war artist. His former head at the Royal College of Art had been one in the First World War, three of his RCA student colleagues (Henry Moore, Eric Ravilious and Edward Bawden) were to be commissioned in 1940, and *Punch* cartoonist Harold Hailstone and his brother Bernard were also official war artists, so he did not lack contacts.

---

7   Though fond of women, Illingworth never married, calling himself 'an optimistic bachelor'. This may have been due to an early rejection. As he later recalled: 'I'm not a misogynist... I knew a delightful girl, born in Hawaii. She was delightful, she lived on a lovely farm in Wales, I adored her. She was five. I was fifteen. I'd made up my mind. When she was 17 and I was 27 I asked her. And she said "no".'

However, though Sir Kenneth Clark (director of the National Gallery, 1934-45) submitted plans for the scheme to the Treasury on the first day of the war, the War Artists' Advisory Committee did not meet for the first time until 23 November 1939 and commissions did not take place until later. So perhaps Illingworth thought this would all be too late. Also, the annual salary was only £650 a year (a third of what he would be paid on the *Daily Mail*) so perhaps his venal streak entered again.

Thus when a job vacancy came up as political cartoonist on the *Daily Mail* – a reserved occupation in wartime – it seemed to be an ideal opportunity to serve his country in the way he knew best. Though he had worked for 13 years as an illustrator Illingworth always wanted to be a political cartoonist again and to be one in wartime was different to his experience with party politics on the *Western Mail*. As he himself said to Keith Mackenzie in 1969: 'It was absolutely easy – there's no doubt about it. We were against Hitler, against Mussolini, against Stalin to start with and then for him immediately as soon as he came in.' He also liked the fact that the cartoonist was always right at the cutting edge of the day's news. As he remarked in the *Observer* in 1970: 'Being a cartoonist is the only job for me...It's like being on the admiral's bridge: you know what's going on and you're in the middle of it. You can't influence the battle but you can take the mickey.' He also had always liked the immediacy of cartoons, describing his work as 'giving people symbols to think with'.

In addition, Illingworth had a head start on his contemporaries in that, unlike most of the cartoonists of his day, he had actually seen many of the Nazi leaders at close quarters in the 1930s when he had visited Garmisch, the winter sports centre near Munich. As he later recalled: 'Hitler, in particular, seemed peculiarly repulsive, with his pasty, flabby face and a certain effeminacy about his movements....The only one for whom I did not feel an instinctive dislike was Goebbels; perhaps it was because his features, though ugly enough, revealed a redeeming sense of humour – though it has since turned out to be a sardonic one.'

Added to which he believed that drawing ability was what counted most in wartime cartooning and that this – together with his personal knowledge of the enemy – meant that he could depict them well without distortion or excessive caricature (which can often prove counter-productive as a weapon). As the distinguished political journalist, Henry Fairlie, remarked in an article about Illingworth in the *Daily Mail* in 1957:

> He delights in observing people and it is this observation which accounts for the fact that, unlike almost every other cartoonist, he does not rely on exaggeration in order to give his caricatures of public figures their point and their impact. He has had the insight to see that everyone is such a caricature of himself in himself that there is no need, if he is acutely observed, to exaggerate.

Keith Mackenzie, another colleague at the *Daily Mail*, also said: 'He is not a cruel or violent man, nor does he do violence to his subjects. His caricatures [are] done with the minimum of distortion, [...] penetrating, delving into the heart and soul – the skull beneath the skin which sets the satirist apart from the cartoonist.'

The *Daily Mail* and its Cartoonists before Illingworth

Before proceeding with Illingworth's wartime career at the *Daily Mail*, it is worth pausing briefly to put his arrival in context by examining the history of the newspaper and its cartoonists.

The *Daily Mail* was launched on 4 May 1896, three years before the start of the Boer War (1899-1902). It was created and owned by Alfred Harmsworth (later Lord Northcliffe), publisher of the weekly *Answers* (1888) and (since 1894) the *Evening News*, the top-selling evening newspaper in London. He also published comic magazines such as *Comic Cuts* and *Illustrated Chips* and in 1908 took over *The Times*.

From its first issue Harmsworth's averred editorial policy for the paper was that 'We don't direct the ordinary man's opinion. We reflect it'. Its co-founder, Kennedy Jones added: 'If Kipling be called the Voice of Empire in English literature, we may fairly claim to [be] the Voice of Empire in London journalism.' Its masthead later included the words 'For King and Empire' and it was in fact read regularly by King George V. Harmsworth also had a simple catchphrase for his journalists: 'Explain, simplify, clarify!' and, of course, what counted for journalists also applied to artists – including cartoonists – in peacetime and in war.

A full-size broadsheet newspaper with advertising on its front page, it was an instant success and immediately entered the record books by having the highest ever circulation in one day by any daily newspaper (397,215 for its first issue). It was later the first daily newspaper ever to sell a million copies and until 1932 it dominated the scene and had the largest circulation of any daily newspaper in the world.

During wartime the *Daily Mail*'s editorial policies were always sympathetic to the fighting man. In the Boer War under editor S.J.Pryor (who was transferred to Cape Town for the duration) the paper offered free Beechams Pills to soldiers on active service in South Africa, and during the First World War it was the official paper to the troops – 10,000 copies being delivered to the Front daily.

It also helped overthrow Asquith and install Lloyd George as minister of munitions, and attacked Kitchener for trying to ban war reporters and for supplying the wrong kind of shells. (Unfortunately such was Kitchener's prestige that this led to a drop in the paper's circulation by 100,000 copies overnight and the *Daily Mail* and *The Times* were both publicly burnt in the Stock Exchange in London and banned from Service clubs in Pall Mall.)

In addition, the *Daily Mail* attacked the Kaiser when other papers were ambivalent about him as he was Victoria's grandson, and claimed in its masthead to be 'The Paper That Foretold the War'. It also printed 'It's a Long Way to Tipperary' on its front page and made it the official anthem of the British Expeditionary Force in the war. Controversially the paper also campaigned for conscription (then unknown in Britain but common elsewhere).

Towards the end of the First World War (February 1918), Northcliffe himself became Director of Propaganda in Enemy Countries and he was the first to promote the use of aerial leaflets being dropped on the enemy. (His brother Harold, meanwhile, was director-general of the Royal Army Clothing Department and in 1917 was appointed air minister.)

The *Daily Mail* was the first paper to employ a team of worldwide correspondents to gather the news from around the globe and among its staff was some of the best journalistic talent of its day. Its writers included Max Beerbohm, Edgar Wallace, G.W.Steevens, Hannen Swaffer, Sir Philip Gibbs (knighted for his reporting of the Great War), Mayson Beeton (son of Mrs Beeton), Rudyard Kipling, Lovat Fraser (who coined the term 'Hun' for the Germans) and Winston Churchill.

In addition it had the world's first ever woman war correspondent (Lady Sarah Wilson in the Boer War) and in the 1940s its star reporter was Rhona Churchill, who has been described in S.J.Taylor's *The Great Outsiders: Northcliffe, Rothermere and the Daily Mail* (1996) as 'the best known woman war correspondent of the Second World War'. It was also a *Daily Mail* photographer, H.A.Mason, who took the iconic picture of St Paul's in the Blitz which was printed on the front page of the paper on 31 December 1940.

On Northcliffe's death in 1922 his brother Harold (by then Lord Rothermere) took over the publishing group. However, such was Rothermere's antagonism to Communism that the *Daily Mail* at first supported Oswald Mosley and the British Union of Fascists (notably in the feature 'Hurrah for the Blackshirts', 8 January 1934) and indeed in the early 1930s the paper was at first pro-Hitler (whom Rothermere had visited a number of times and corresponded with from 1933 to 1938). Partly because of this the *Daily Mail* ceased to be the top-selling daily newspaper in Britain and in 1933 was overtaken by the *Daily Express*.

Though the *Daily Mail* was not the first national daily paper in Britain to carry political cartoons, it might well have been. Before it was launched no less than 65 experimental four-page issues had been produced. One of these (Thursday 16 April 1896) had a remarkably modern-looking masthead and beneath it, on the front page, a large four-column cartoon on the Boer War by 'Rip' (Roland Pretty Hill, c.1866-1949). Entitled 'Will Little Trilby Come?' it featured Joseph Chamberlain (Secretary for the Colonies) as Svengali trying to hypnotise Boer leader Paul Kruger, dressed as Trilby O'Ferrall (from George Du Maurier's 1894 novel *Trilby*), into singing 'Rule Britannia'.

It was also 'Rip' who drew the first political cartoon ever to appear in the *Daily Mail* ('The Mystic East: The Busy West', 3 August 1896). It featured Prime Minister Lord Salisbury welcoming China's viceroy to Britain and appeared alongside an article entitled 'Political Cartoons, Their Rise and Progress', which began:

One of the most interesting developments of modern times is the art of political cartooning. [...] Indeed it is said on excellent authority that politicians consider it such a mark of honour to be cartooned that many send their best photographs to the well-known cartoonists, and it is vigorously maintained by many that a politician does not amount to much until he has been cartooned. After that distinction he is supposed to have advanced several steps and to have arrived at a distinction that makes him a force of some moment.

The Boer War led to considerable interest in political cartoons and the *Daily Mail* occasionally reprinted work by Sir John Tenniel of *Punch* and Francis Carruthers Gould of the *Westminster Gazette* (who in 1887, when at the *Pall Mall Gazette*, had become Britain's first ever staff political cartoonist on a daily newspaper). However, most cartoons published in the *Daily Mail* at this time were foreign drawings reproduced under the title 'As Others See Us' (pointing out the brutality, lack of imagination and ignorance of Britain of misguided foreigners). 'Plucking the British Bird' (25 December 1896), for example – from the German satirical magazine *Lustige Blätter* – depicted a smug John Bull as a strutting turkey with Boer leader Paul Kruger attempting to pull out a tail-feather marked 'Cape Colony' and US President Grover Cleveland tugging on another marked 'Canada' (others were labelled 'India' and 'Egypt').

It was not until the First World War that the newspaper used cartoons with any regularity. Though the *Daily Mail* still did not have a staff cartoonist it reprinted drawings by the Dutchman Louis Raemaekers (1869-1956) of *De Telegraaf* and by 'Poy' from the *Daily Mail*'s sister paper, the *Evening News*. Northcliffe also expressed great admiration for the work of Will Dyson (1880-1938) of the *Daily Herald* (this 'young man with the most virile style of any British cartoonist') and on 1 January 1915 cancelled all advertisements for the entire back page of the paper (thereby losing considerable revenue) to reprint Dyson's 'Wonders of Science!' drawing from his book *Kultur Cartoons* (1915) so that it 'occupies a larger space than any cartoon has ever before been given in a British newspaper'.

'Poy' (Percy Fearon, 1874-1948) had joined the *Evening News* in 1913 and for more than 20 years (until 1935) his cartoons were often reproduced the next day in the pages of its morning sister paper, the *Daily Mail* (during the First World War he also drew for the *Weekly Dispatch*, which was part of the same group). Then in 1935, in an effort to boost flagging sales of the *Daily Mail*, he moved from the *Evening News* (being replaced by Bert Thomas) and became the first ever staff political cartoonist on the *Daily Mail*, remaining in this job until 1938. A good caricaturist, cartoonist and occasional journalist, Philip Connard RA once described him as 'the prettiest draughtsman of all cartoonists'. However, he greatly simplified his style when he joined the *Evening News* and *Daily Mail* (as would Illingworth himself), both for speed (and clarity) of production and to suit the tone of the papers.

Other cartoonists working at the *Daily Mail* before Illingworth's arrival included Tom Webster (1886-1962) who had joined the *Evening News* as sports cartoonist in 1918, moving to the *Daily Mail* the following year and remaining with the paper for more than 20 years (he left in 1940). By 1924 Webster had become the highest paid cartoonist (of any sort) in world, earning an estimated £20,000 a year (then an enormous sum). In October 1924 he and Poy had their drawings illustrating the election results projected onto a giant screen at the Albert Hall before an invited audience of 10,000 *Daily Mail* readers, and during the 1929 election Webster's cartoons were projected onto an equally large screen giving the results in Trafalgar Square

There was also the pocket (or single-column) cartoonist 'Neb' (Ronald Niebour) who had joined the paper as an illustrator in 1938 and turned to pocket cartoons when war broke out. (He continued to work for the *Daily Mail* until his retirement in 1960.) Another was the Hungarian/German expatriate 'Vicky' (Victor Weisz, 1913-66), who had drawn a series of 'Funny Figures' (illustrated statistics) for the *Daily Mail* in 1937 and also illustrated the gossip column 'Almost in Confidence' for the *Sunday Dispatch* (formerly the *Weekly Dispatch*). Finally Julian Phipps (1907-91, later art editor of Associated Newspapers) had joined the *Daily Mail* in 1929 and stayed for more than 11 years, working as a journalist (illustrating his own articles) and producing such (usually single-panel) cartoon features as 'Laugh with Phipps' and 'Crazy News Reel' (1937-8). He returned to the paper after the war as a fashion artist.

As for strip cartoons, the very popular 'Teddy Tail' series featuring a mouse with a knot in his tail first appeared on 5 April 1915, created, written and drawn by Charles Folkard. (It proved to be so successful that the *Daily Express* started the now much better-known 'Rupert Bear' in competition.) 'Teddy Tail' was later taken over by Folkard's son Harry and then, from 1933 to 1940, by Herbert Foxwell (Foxwell was called up in 1939 and died in 1943). Another children's strip was 'The Nipper' by Brian White (1902-84) which ran from 30 August 1933 to 1941 and then from 1946 to 1947. It featured a baby ('nipper' is slang for a child) and was usually speechless.

The *Daily Mail* and the Second World War

This, then, was the world that Illingworth was contemplating entering when 'Poy' retired and the *Daily Mail* advertised for a political cartoonist. At the suggestion of his agent, Illingworth agreed to apply for the job and asked Owen Aves to submit two of his cartoons amongst a group by 'unknown' artists.[8] They were drawn in a simpler style than that which he had used for *Punch* and his illustration work and he used the pseudonym 'MacGregor' (his mother's maiden name) in the belief that his (by then well known) work for *Punch* and other magazines would count against him in Fleet Street.

Illingworth's ruse was detected by the deputy editor, Gordon Beckles, but he got the job and later declared: 'Thank God I succeeded.' His first drawing 'Feeding Time' appeared on Monday 30 October 1939 – nearly two months after the start of the Second World War and during the relatively quiet period known as the Phoney War. Before long he had settled into work at the *Daily Mail*'s offices in Northcliffe House, just off Fleet Street, as the newspaper's first ever staff political cartoonist in wartime.

He was paid £1500 a year (rising to £2000 after three months) and remained as political cartoonist through eight editors (ending with Arthur Brittenden) until 1969 when he retired (his last cartoon, 'They're Off', was published on 22 December that year), being succeeded by Wally Fawkes (Trog). He also worked for the paper under two successive proprietors: Harold Harmsworth (Lord Rothermere), who died on 27 November 1940 – thus Illingworth only worked for one year under his regime – and his son Esmond (later 2nd Viscount Rothermere).

Illingworth drew four cartoons a week for the *Daily Mail* (normally published on Monday, Wednesday, Friday and Saturday, but sometimes on other days as well) and his wartime drawings usually occupied a rectangle at the top of the leader page (page 6) to the right of the leader itself and with its right edge ranged right on the newspaper's right textual margins. At first it extended across three columns (roughly 7 inches wide by 5 inches deep) above a series of regular feature articles written by *Mail* staffers (e.g. 'I See Life' by Charles Graves, 'Lane-Norcott's War Fare' or 'Down on the Farm' by Pat Murphy) or above special reports by guest freelancers. Between the cartoon and the leader there was usually a feature commenting on the day's news (e.g. 'The Way the War is Going' by the *Daily Mail*'s diplomatic correspondent, Wilson Broadbent). Thus the cartoon was very closely linked to the content of the texts around it – especially the leader and the adjoining political commentary column.

Illingworth's drawings continued to appear throughout the war, despite the fact that by the end of 1940 paper rationing had reduced the *Daily Mail* to six pages. The resulting premium on space meant that other pictorial features – such as children's cartoons, continuity strips and sports cartoons – were later dropped. However, Illingworth's cartoon remained, a testament to its importance.

Illingworth's small office at the *Daily Mail* (seen in the Ministry of Information photograph of him on page 10) was Room 60 on the fourth floor of Northcliffe House on the corner of Whitefriars Street and Tudor Street and close to Temple Chambers in the Temple complex where he kept a room to draw his *Punch* cartoon (*Punch* then had offices nearby at 10 Bouverie Street). As Fenn Sherie recorded in a wartime article on Illingworth for the *Strand Magazine* (1941): 'There, in a top-floor room, regardless of sirens and roof-spotters, he spends his mornings turning out, perhaps, half a dozen rough sketches for discussion at the midday conference, and returns in the afternoon to produce, in a couple of hours, one of the finely finished cartoons that provide daily delight for a vast public.'

His daily routine was much the same during the war as it was 30 years later (as described in 1969 by Keith Mackenzie):

---

8   Illingworth's illustrator friend Clive Uptton (also agented by Aves) had already been turned down for the job through lack of experience as a political cartoonist (he later became daily political cartoonist on the *Daily Sketch* and *Sunday Graphic* from 1940 to 1942).

Feeding Time
Daily Mail, 30 October 1939

Illingworth's first cartoon for the *Daily Mail*, in which bureaucrats are seen herding blindfolded businessmen into the clutches of the monocled Rt Hon. Pool Octopus ('Petrol' has already succumbed), appeared on page 6 of the paper. It very much reflects the comments in the nearby leader column condemning the government's system of universal control where everything is 'pooled' in the interest of the war effort. Even the image of the octopus is supplied in the leader-writer's text: 'How many controllers are damming the flow of trade? How many committees are telling businessmen how to run business? What is the cost to the country of this bloated octopus? What is the effect on prices?'

Illingworth's day starts when he listens to the early morning's news and studies all the morning's papers. By the time he arrives at Northcliffe House several possibilities are taking shape in his head. Before lunch a number of linear roughs are presented to the editor and the chosen idea and appropriate shape decided upon. With a roughly pencilled design on a virgin sheet of board, the real work starts after lunch when the situation, likeness and background will be rapidly drawn in with a fine pen, strengthened by brush, chalk, mechanical tint or wash. He doesn't use photographic reference much; like all good draughtsmen he draws things well because he 'knows' them [...]. Corrections and deletions being completed with Process White and razor blade, the drawing will then be ready for the Process Department from whom will emerge a line block ready for printing.

It took approximately four hours to complete his daily cartoon and shortly before, or soon after 7.30 p.m. (the deadline for the *Daily Mail*'s Scottish edition) the finished drawing was handed over to the production department. However, once finished, Illingworth seemed to have had no further interest in his work. As Keith Mackenzie later observed: 'By a curious quirk, once the drawing is out of his hands he never wants to see it in print and cannot bear to open the paper with his drawing in it.'

The routine for his weekly *Punch* work was slightly different. The *Punch* table met on Wednesdays and after their deliberations Illingworth had 36 hours to produce his drawing in time to be sent to the press on Friday for the following week's issue. A contemporary account of Illingworth's wartime routine appeared in *London Opinion* in December 1941 where Percy V. Bradshaw (himself briefly a former *Daily Mail* artist under Northcliffe) explained that the secret of how Illingworth could turn from the 'leisurely character drawing' of his illustration work to the 'swift comment' of the daily newspaper political cartoonist was 'a combination of great artistic ability – and a talent for doing without sleep':

> Illingworth's toughest period of the week begins usually on those Thursday mornings, when he has a *Punch* cartoon and two *Daily Mail* cartoons to produce before Saturday.
>
> When you go to bed on Thursday night, you might like to give a thought to Illingworth, busy in his room at the *Daily Mail*. When you wake up on Friday morning he will still be working, and, with intervals for a breakfast at a Fleet Street milk bar and lunch – perhaps – at the Savoy, he will continue to dispense with sleep all through the day.
>
> During the 'Blitz' periods the nightly programme was interrupted by helping to put out incendiaries on the *Daily Mail* roof – and, perhaps, by the need to scrap a cartoon owing to a sudden change in the world's news.
>
> Does all this sound like a grim and ghastly life? Believe me, Illingworth doesn't think so.
>
> He revels in it. [...] He loves the excitement of a newspaper office, the thrill of being in the centre of things. It seems to keep him fresh and young, fit and happy.

Illingworth usually liked to spend a whole day on his *Punch* drawing in his small garret room in Temple Chambers, but sometimes he ran out of time and had to finish it in the *Daily Mail*'s office. One such occasion revealed Illingworth's immense patience, as fellow *Daily Mail* journalist Pat Murphy (who shared an office with Illingworth) later recalled. He had nearly completed a scraperboard cartoon for *Punch* with a theme based on Shelley's poem 'The Cloud' and illustrating the line 'like a swarm of golden bees...' when disaster struck.

> He had drawn about 650 bees with their four wings and six legs and a dense complicated countryside background. Suddenly a gust of wind whipped the drawing off his easel and out of the window. He walked over to the balustrade and peered down, muttering: 'I bet it goes face down.' It not only went face down but a *Daily Mail* van drove over it, destroying the six or seven hours' work, for it was nearly finished....Leslie pulled out another huge board from his quiver of them and saying: 'Oh! Aye, start all over again' began to do exactly that.

Throughout the London Blitz, after his daytime work for the *Daily Mail* and *Punch* and others, Illingworth also served in the Home Guard in the evenings. He was first attached to the Local Defence Volunteers and later (1942-4) was on night duty on an anti-aircraft rocket battery stationed in Hyde Park, near his home.

In about 1940 Illingworth and Enid Ratcliff moved to a flat above the Scotch House at 14 Park Mansions, Knightsbridge, London, SW7 (which they kept until 1963) and they later also took possession of a country home, The White Bungalow at Povey Cross in Horley, Sussex (c.1940-46), originally bought by Enid with an inheritance when her father died and used as a hostel for evacuee children from London. (Enid became a Land Army girl when the war started and later worked for the art agency, Clement Danes, where she became Illingworth's agent after Owen Aves died.) Illingworth was always very generous with his rooms and allowed refugee journalists to stay in the Knightsbridge flat, including the Czech cartoonist Stephen Roth, who was then drawing sports cartoons for the *Daily Mail* and later became political cartoonist on the *Sunday Pictorial*.

During the war years Illingworth produced a total of 1018 cartoons for the *Daily Mail* alone. His output was almost completely uninterrupted throughout the conflict – except when he was (briefly) on holiday. Also, though he produced three or four rough drawings each day from which the editor chose one, he was always adamant that his ideas for his *Daily Mail* cartoons were entirely his own: 'I've never been told what to do. Never, never, never. The

Lament for the Stand-Down
Daily Mail, 4 December 1944

After working in the daytime at the *Daily Mail* Illingworth served in the Home Guard. This nostalgic and at the same time ironic cartoon shows Illingworth carrying out his duties as a night-time anti-aircraft gunner in Home Guard Battery Z (a rocket battery) before it was 'stood down' (disbanded) in 1944. It was one of two cartoons on the topic of the stand-down which Illingworth drew for the *Daily Mail* that day.

best editor is a man that will look at your roughs and say "Oh, wonderful! Good! That's the one I want".'

That the ideas for his *Punch* drawings were the result of teamwork is certainly no revelation – since the beginning of the magazine in 1841, the theme for the big full-page cartoon was decided by a staff committee and then the artist was asked to draw it. Over the years Leech, Tenniel, Sambourne, Partridge and others all worked this way. However, there is no indication that Illingworth's daily newspaper work was anything other than his own. Indeed, there would have been little time for consultation on a daily paper in peacetime, let alone in wartime.

This is not to say that his *Daily Mail* cartoons were not occasionally tinkered with by other staff members. A particular case in point is an untitled drawing (6 November 1942) featuring a dead German who faces right on the original but was 'flopped' (reversed) on the printed version. As a result, Illingworth had to reletter the words '"Invincible Germans" Myth', swap the wristwatch to the figure's other arm, and redraw the swastika on his shirt.

Captions were another area where change often occurred. Illingworth was quite open about this as was revealed in a wartime feature on him by Charles Graves in the *Daily Mail* (14 March 1941): 'If you ask him [Illingworth] how he works, he will tell you that he reads the newspapers and creates concrete symbols of the news. His trouble, he says, is that he doesn't think in words, and he just can't do snappy captions.' An example of this is the cartoon for 27 May 1940 (see page 47) for which at least four alternative captions were produced. Examination of the original drawings for Illingworth's cartoons also reveals a number of occasions when his spelling was corrected.

In some exceptional cases a few of Illingworth's cartoons appear not to have met with the full approval of the editor (or art editor). For example, on 15 August 1941, two different Illingworth cartoons were published on the subject of Anglo-US solidarity – the Manchester edition of the paper (drawn first) had 'The Builders Meet' while the London edition had 'The Torch'. On another occasion (13 April 1945), his original cartoon – showing a German civilian welcoming the Allies with an outstretched bloody hand – only appeared in the first London edition. However, this may have been because a similar cartoon by Illingworth had been published by the *Daily Mail* the previous year ('No Heinrich, it won't wash', 19 September 1944) with Allied troops refusing to shake the bloody hand of a German civilian who calls 'My liberator!'

It is also possible that sometimes Illingworth's drawing was dropped because the same idea had been used by a cartoonist on a rival newspaper. However, this did not seem to have prevented publication of Illingworth's 'Lower Away!' (3 November 1943) after the Moscow Conference. In this a huge block of stone labelled 'Anglo-Russian-American Accord – the Foundation Stone of a Lasting Peace' descends on Hitler and the Nazis. On the very same day Sidney Strube's cartoon 'Foundation Stone' appeared in the *Daily Express* with a similar block of stone (labelled 'Moscow Conference') squashing Hitler and the Nazis.

There were even occasions when, ironically, Illingworth's drawing was too good to be used. As an article in *Newsweek* (17 April 1944) remarked: 'Occasionally editor Robert J.Prew and features editor Sidney Hornblow choose a rough draft over the finished drawing because Illingworth's passion for detail sometimes destroys the flair of the original.'

Illingworth's tremendous draughtsmanship was universally acknowledged. This was evident, the Blitz notwithstanding, in every one of his wartime cartoons, whether they were for the *Daily Mail*, *Punch* or government propaganda departments. Julian Phipps (1907-91), a fellow wartime cartoonist on the *Daily Mail* – and later art editor of Associated Newspapers (1953-70) – remarked that as well as being 'a political observer of global stature' Illingworth was a draughtsman 'of consummate gifts...the most technically accomplished pen in Britain'.

Many others have added their praise. Draper Hill – the distinguished American political cartoonist, art historian and biographer of James Gillray – has called Illingworth 'simply the finest draughtsman of our time to have devoted himself to editorial caricature'. In the view of Malcolm Muggeridge (*Punch* editor, 1953-7) he was 'an incomparable black-and-white artist' and William Hewison (*Punch* art editor, 1960-84) described him as having a 'faultless pen-and-ink technique, a technique which is essentially naturalistic yet masterly in its variety of textures, arrangement of tones, and subtle atmospheric perspective'. Nicholas Garland OBE, political cartoonist of the *Daily Telegraph*, has described him as 'the last of a great line of black and white draughtsmen... There is no mystery about his work. It is just superb'.

Propaganda Work

Most of the wartime political cartoonists (including Illingworth) did a fair amount of propaganda work for the Ministry of Information and other government departments. However, perhaps for obvious reasons, this was usually anonymous. That said, the Public Record Office in Kew, Surrey, does have (indexed as by 'Illingwroth' though clearly signed 'Illingworth') a large colour sketch (15 x 12in) dating from about 1940 and showing Churchill as John Bull holding a rifle with fixed bayonet. His back is against the wall, climbing over which from behind can be seen Britain's allies in military uniform. (This drawing is similar in concept to his *Daily Mail* cartoon of 16 February 1942 – published after the fall of Singapore – with John Bull as a British Tommy with his back to a wall labelled 'Dunkirk Mood'.)

The Ministry of Information was founded in March 1918 with the aim of producing propaganda material against the Germans but also for Home Front consumption (Hitler remarked on its success in *Mein Kampf*). In 1939 it was resurrected and located in London University's Senate House building in Malet Street near the British Museum and backing onto Russell Square with a separate office – the Political Warfare Executive (producing so-called 'black propaganda') – at Woburn Abbey in Bedfordshire. In an official memo its main duty was stated as being 'the dissemination of truth to attack the enemy in the minds of the public'.

The first minister of information (1939-40) was Lord Macmillan (Hugh Macmillan, 1873-1952). Then, in the spring of 1940 (after a brief spell by Sir John Reith), he was succeeded by Alfred Duff Cooper, aided by his parliamentary secretary Harold Nicolson as director with Walter Monckton as his deputy. Rear Admiral Thomson was the chief press censor, and its art director (who eventually dealt with some 70-odd artists) was Edwin Embleton (formerly of Odhams).

At its peak its general staff amounted to some 3000 employees including postal censorship workers and a number of specialists from the press, radio and advertising. Amongst these were such celebrated names as the art historian Kenneth Clark, the BBC's Guy Burgess (later revealed as a Russian spy) and the future Poet Laureate John Betjeman.

In July 1941, after much criticism of the department (see Illingworth's *Daily Mail* cartoon 'Dead Weight', 2 July 1941, reproduced on page 72), Nicolson was sacked and the MOI was reorganised with Churchill's close friend Brendan Bracken replacing Duff Cooper.

That Illingworth contributed cartoons to the Political Warfare Executive is confirmed by his statement (in an interview by the cartoonist Smilby in the 1970s) that during the war he drew cartoons showing 'Germans fucking Italians' wives' for aerial propaganda leaflets. This work may have been linked to that of the German-born cartoonist Walter Goetz (who had drawn strip cartoons for the *Express* since 1934) who, amongst other projects, organised and contributed drawings to the *Luftpost* aerial leaflet series for the PWE.

Though unsigned, Illingworth also drew cartoon posters for the Ministry of War Transport – such as 'Whew! That's Quicker Turnround' (5 September 1941),[9] one of a series to encourage the public to speed up the loading and unloading of goods – and the Ministry of Information (e.g. 'Just a Good Afternoon's Work', 8 June 1942).[10] In addition, the photograph of him reproduced on page 10 was part of a wartime information package the MOI distributed about how a typical daily paper works.

Illingworth also drew illustrations for the Royal Navy publication *Dittybox: The Navy's Own Magazine* and a number of his *Daily Mail* cartoons were reproduced in *Le Courrier de l'Air*. This London-produced aerial propaganda newspaper (and its smaller companion *Revue de la Presse Libre*) was dropped by the RAF over occupied France (500,000 copies of each issue were printed). As well as work by Lancaster, Kem, Low, Strube and Vicky, a number of Illingworth's *Daily Mail* cartoons appeared in its pages with their captions translated into French. Among these was the drawing from 24 October 1941 (see page 75). A special supplement, *Le Courrier de l'Air Illustré* from early 1943 (No.5) contains two cartoons by Illingworth – 23 January (retitled 'Gare au Moustique') and 29 January (see page 107).

---

9 Proof of this being by Illingworth is a photo in the Illingworth Papers at the British Cartoon Archive at the University of Kent which shows him sitting at an easel and completing the drawing.

10 Though classified as 'Artist Unknown' by the PRO, the original drawing has Illingworth's name on the back.

Another wartime foreign-language aerial newspaper which was produced in Britain and which featured British cartoons was the two-page *De Vliegende Hollander* (The Flying Dutchman), 600,000 of which were dropped by the RAF over occupied Holland. At least one of Illingworth's cartoons, 'In Column of Rout' (*Daily Mail*, 12 June 1944) was reproduced in its pages (in the issue for 22 June 1944). Another of Illingworth's wartime *Daily Mail* cartoons (30 May 1940) was republished as a postcard (translated into Portuguese) by the British Embassy in Lisbon, Portugal, and distributed throughout Europe (see page 49).

Other Uses of Illingworth's Wartime Cartoons

From January 1944 until at least November 1945 many of Illingworth's cartoons were republished (slightly reduced in size) in the transatlantic edition of the *Daily Mail*. This gave him a huge overseas readership. In 1944 an article in *Newsweek* reprinted his cartoon 'Up the Connoisseurs!' (18 February 1944) and described Illingworth as 'one of Britain's best known cartoonists – perhaps second only to the world-famous David Low…The tremendous national circulation of the *Daily Mail* (most recent ABC figure: 1,416,192) plus reprint privileges extended by its transatlantic edition, give Illingworth a British-American audience rivalling the estimated 200,000,000 of Low.'

A number of his drawings were also reprinted in US magazines and newspapers (for example in *Time* magazine on 20 March 1944) and soon after the war Illingworth's cartoon 'The Atom-Squatters' (30 October 1945) was reproduced over half the front page of the *Washington Daily News*.

In addition his *Daily Mail* drawings regularly featured in the *War Illustrated* weekly magazine throughout the conflict and appeared in wartime books such as the Associated Press's own collection, *400 Famous Cartoons by Five Famous Cartoonists from the Daily Mail, Evening News, Sunday Dispatch* (1944). More than 70 of his drawings were reproduced along with those by Sidney Moon (fl.1930s-after 1955), Joe Lee (1901-74) and pocket cartoonists Neb and Harold Gittins (fl.1930s-after 1950). The front cover, depicting the smiling Allied leaders Stalin, Churchill and Roosevelt, was designed by Illingworth. This collection also included a cartoon that proved to be prophetic. After Chamberlain claimed in the House of Commons on 6 May 1940 that Hitler had 'Missed the Bus' when he invaded Denmark and Norway, Illingworth drew a powerful criticism of this in his cartoon 'The Bus'. Three days later Chamberlain resigned (see page 43).[11]

Some of Illingworth's *Daily Mail* drawings were also included in wartime cartoon anthologies such as S.-L.Hourmouzios' *Salute to Greece: An Anthology of Cartoons Published in the British Press* (1942) – see pages 61 and 62 – and *Verdensdramaet i Karikaturer, 1939-1945* (Copenhagen, 1945), a large Danish international collection of cartoons (featuring drawings from Allied and Axis publications) edited by S.P. Bahnsen and P.A. Fogelström. There were also popular wartime exhibitions of his original *Daily Mail* cartoons in department stores such as Kendal Milne & Co. in Deansgate, Manchester (1940) and Lewis's Stores, Glasgow (1943).

Illingworth's work also had a notable impact on the Nazis themselves. Proof of this is the fact that one of Illingworth's cartoons – about the Japanese invasion of New Guinea – was reprinted in the weekly *Das Reich* in 1942 as part of a special feature attacking the *Daily Mail* (see page 84). Cuttings of his *Daily Mail* drawings were also found in German files after the war. One of these, featuring his cartoon 'One They Can't Lay' (29 March 1944) had been carefully filed and classified by Goebbels' propaganda ministry as item No.14947 (see page 125). Another cutting found in Berlin was 'On His Last Leg' (14 January 1944) which showed a sweating tiny Hitler in a basement with his left leg caught in a steel man-trap labelled 'Dnieper' struggling to put out the fuse on a huge barrel of 'Anglo-US Invasion Dynamite'.[12]

---

11 A similar incident occurred three years later. On 21 September 1943 Illingworth drew the British Cabinet in a classroom scene ('Look Out Chaps…The Head!') in which the chancellor of the exchequer, Sir Kingsley Wood, was depicted with a halo. A few hours after its publication came news of the chancellor's death.

12 One of his *Punch* cartoons about the invasion of Finland ('Who Aids?', 22 February 1940) was also incorporated into a cartoon by the German artist Garvens and reprinted in *Kladderadatsch* in June 1941.

It is perhaps appropriate that the cover drawing of this collection of wartime cartoons from the artists of the Associated Newspapers group should have been specially drawn by its senior political cartoonist, Leslie Illingworth. One of his *Daily Mail* cartoons ('Nearing the Showdown', 7 November 1941) also appears on the back cover.

Conclusion

After the war Illingworth continued to work for the *Daily Mail*, remaining at the newspaper for 30 years (and through eight editorships) – long after all his wartime rivals had moved on from their papers, retired or died. From 1957 onwards he alternated his cartoons with those of Emmwood (John Musgrave-Wood, 1915-99) and sometimes Chrys (George Chrystal, 1921-72) and also contributed occasional articles, often illustrating his own international travel pieces (e.g. 'Illingworth at Large' in the 1960s).

In addition he later worked for a short time as political cartoonist on the weekly *Sunday Dispatch* (part of the same group), until the paper closed in 1961 and in January 1963 he was commissioned by *Time* magazine to produce a colour cover which summed up the situation of Britain that year. On the death of Sir Bernard Partridge in 1945 he had become the main cartoonist on *Punch* (notably drawing a highly controversial portrait of the ageing Prime Minister Winston Churchill in 1954), but did little work for the magazine from 1957 (when Malcolm Muggeridge left as editor) to 1962 and then alternated his drawings with those of Norman Mansbridge (1911-93) until he finally left in 1968.

On 22 December 1969 Illingworth published his last cartoon for the *Daily Mail* and retired to his smallholding in Robertsbridge, Sussex (bought in 1946). However, he later returned to Fleet Street to work as guest political cartoonist on the *News of the World* (1974-6). Voted Political and Social Cartoonist of the Year by the Cartoonists' Club of Great Britain in 1962, he was one of the founder members and the first president of the British Cartoonists' Association when it was formed in 1966. In this capacity he was involved in 'Drawn and Quartered: The World of the British Newspaper Cartoon, 1720-1970' a major exhibition held at the National Portrait Gallery in London and opened by Princess Margaret (see page 77). Solo exhibitions of his own work followed in Boston, Massachusetts (1970) at the Arts Club in London (1971) and (posthumously) at the National Library of Wales in Aberystwyth (2002). He also contributed to '*Not By Appointment*' (1977) an exhibition of royal cartoons held at the London Press Club in Fleet Street which was opened by Prince Charles. Illingworth was a member of the Toby Club, the Chelsea Arts Club and the Royal Automobile Club, and met a great many politicians and international celebrities through his work (including US Presidents L.B.Johnson and Richard Nixon), many of whom collected his original drawings. In 1975 he was awarded an Honorary D.Litt degree from the University of Kent, home of the British Cartoon Archive.

In 1979, after an operation for gallstones, Illingworth suffered a stroke. He died in Hastings Hospital on 20 December that year and after a funeral service in Saleshurst Church, Sussex, on 31 December 1979 was cremated in Hastings. A memorial service was later held in St Bride's Church, Fleet Street, on 26 February 1980.

Towards the end of the Great War, the US Senator Hiram Johnson famously declared that: 'The first casualty when war comes is truth' (1917). However, during the Second World War – despite the best and worst efforts of newspaper editors, government censors and propagandists to interfere – Illingworth and his fellow political cartoonists did their utmost to communicate that truth (or at least their perception of it) to the readers of their newspapers.

Two decades before Illingworth's death, his friend and neighbour in Robertsbridge, *Punch* editor Malcolm Muggeridge, described this aspect of the work of the political cartoonist:

A satirist, by the nature of the case, cannot but give offence. Truth is his medium, and truth hurts. If he muffles or evades it, he ceases to be a satirist – which is why he is a dangerous instrument of propaganda, and a poor servant of conformity. An untruthful satirist is as inconceivable as a colour-blind artist or a tone-deaf musician. This is particularly true of the graphic satirist, of the caricaturist or cartoonist. He has to crystallise a moment of bitter awareness of man's inhumanity, greed, hypocrisy, futility. [...] On the other hand, the graphic satirist has his reward. It is in his power to capture, in a way which is possible in no other medium, the fleeting, dancing particles of history. Words which belong to the moment for the most part perish with the moment.[13]

This power to capture 'the fleeting, dancing particles of history' is what the political cartoonist possesses both in peacetime and in war, but it is in wartime that the exercise of this power is often most successful. It is thus perhaps no surprise to learn that a number of British cartoonists (including Illingworth) were on the Gestapo's Death List during the Second World War – had the Germans succeeded in occupying Britain they would have been amongst the first to be shot. Though political cartoonists in wartime may not win medals for their work, and are usually far from the Front Line, they are certainly worthy of our respect.

The quotation at the beginning of this introduction, from a Boer War issue of the *Daily Mail* in 1899, said that 'a political cartoonist is the rarest of all artists' and expressed the hope that the conflict would make 'a great reputation' for one of them. During the Second World War nearly half a century later, as the drawings in this book demonstrate, Leslie Illingworth of the *Daily Mail* achieved that goal and became one of the finest war cartoonists of his time.

13 Introduction to *Vicky's World* (1959).

1939

I T IS NOW WIDELY ACCEPTED that the seeds of the Second World War were sown in the ruins of the Great War that ended almost two decades earlier. At the 1919 Peace Conference in Versailles Palace, near Paris, the victorious Allies – led by Britain, France and the USA – forced a defeated Germany to surrender large areas of its territory and to pay huge sums in compensation. However, Germany's shattered economy could not cope and when it began to default on repayments, French and Belgian troops were sent in to occupy the important industrial area of the Ruhr, leading to further financial difficulties for Germany.

It was against this background that political unrest began to simmer and by 1930 the National Socialist German Workers' Party – the Nazis – had begun to make their mark, blaming Germany's ills on the betrayal at Versailles and using scapegoats such as Communism and Judaism. The Nazis eventually became the single largest party in Germany and on 30 January 1933 their leader, Adolf Hitler, was appointed chancellor (prime minister) of Germany. After consolidating his position Hitler then began to implement his policy of seeking *Lebensraum* (living space) for the German-speaking peoples who he viewed as being an Aryan master-race. This resulted in Germany annexing Austria. To avoid conflict so soon after the horrors of the First World War, Britain's Prime Minister Neville Chamberlain played the role of peace-maker at any cost and at a conference in Munich agreed to the occupation of the German-speaking Sudetenland area of Czechoslovakia. However, when Hitler then marched into Prague in 1939 and started to threaten Poland as well – at the same time forming pacts with Mussolini's Fascist Italy and Stalin's Communist Soviet Union – Britain and its allies abandoned their policy of appeasement. When Germany invaded Poland in a sudden heavily armoured attack, on 1 September 1939, Britain declared war.

After the invasion of Poland there was very little fighting in Europe in 1939 until the USSR attacked Finland in November. This period of comparative peace was known as the 'Phoney War' but it was only to prove the lull before the storm. In fact, large numbers of German troops had begun to mass on the country's Dutch and Belgian borders.

In this cartoon by Illingworth, the third he drew for the *Daily Mail* and his first ever to feature Goering and Von Ribbentrop, Hitler is shown surrounded by advisers giving him conflicting opinions. At the back can be seen Goering and von Ribbentrop (German foreign minister).

'Why not an offensive today?... Wait until the spring...
Russian gold is behind us... Germany is bankrupt...
Why not bomb Britain?... there might be reprisals...
The workers are for you, Führer!... there is unrest in the factories'
Daily Mail, 2 November 1939

Previous page: **The Non-Start Express** *Daily Mail*, 15 November 1939

'What, don't you recognise me, Führer?'
Daily Mail, 10 November 1939

On the 16th anniversary of the failed 1923 Munich *putsch*, in which the Nazis had tried to take power in Bavaria, Adolf Hitler made a speech in a Munich beer hall and left early to catch the Berlin train. Minutes later a powerful explosion from a bomb planted close to where he had been speaking killed eight people and injured 60.

The original title for the cartoon was 'Why so startled, Führer? Don't you recognize one of your first members of the party?' Presumably the change of title was made by the editor or art editor after Illingworth had handed it in and seems to support Keith Mackenzie's later observation: 'By a curious quirk, once the drawing is out of his hands he never wants to see it in print and cannot bear to open the paper with his drawing in it.' This was the second of Illingworth's drawings to appear in *400 Famous Cartoons* (1944, see page 28) and the sixth in the book. The first (not counting the self-portrait in its introduction, see page 16) was 'Chapter One' (1 June 1940, reproduced on page 37).

'What, me? No, I never <u>touch</u> goldfish'
Daily Mail, 17 November 1939

After the division of Poland between the USSR and Germany and the attack on Finland by the Soviet Union, the natural thought of the world's governments was 'Where next?' The answer seemed to be the Balkan states. Illingworth has Hitler and Stalin as two smug cats sitting by a goldfish bowl marked 'Balkans' and wondering which one to eat next. The fish are labelled Bulgaria, Greece, Romania and Yugoslavia.

Though one of Illingworth's best known war cartoons, and one of his own personal favourites as a drawing, the design was completely accidental. As he said in an interview in 1976: 'I was fiddling, doing little drawings of cats, goldfish and bowls, and suddenly there it was. I was not thinking of them at all, I was thinking of a little girl for whom I wanted to draw the cats and goldfish.'

'And I've plenty more pockets'
Daily Mail, 16 December 1939

Though the Phoney War continued on the mainland of Europe, a very real war was happening at sea. This drawing comments on the Battle of the River Plate when the famous German pocket battleship the *Admiral Graf Spee* was scuttled by its captain outside Montevideo harbour at the mouth of the Rio de la Plata in neutral Uruguay, in the mistaken belief that is was facing a hugely superior British naval force. (A pocket battleship was one built so small that it appeared to fit in with the 10,000-ton limit imposed on Germany by the Versailles Treaty, though in fact it was more heavily armed than much bigger vessels.)

OH, HERMANN, BUT IT LOOKS SWEET! AND FOR EVERY OTHER SCUTTLING VICTORY WE CAN ADD A TEENY-WEENY LUMP OF ERSATZ COAL

Raeder

The Order of the Silver Scuttle
Daily Mail, 20 December 1939

Another view of the scuttling of the *Graf Spee*. In this cartoon – featuring Hitler, Goering and Admiral Raeder (commander-in-chief of German naval forces – his first of only two appearances in wartime cartoons by Illingworth) – Illingworth plays on the ambiguity of the word 'scuttle' and alludes to *Ersatz* (or substitute) materials that Germany was forced to use because of the blockade of supplies by the Allies. The cartoon appeared alongside an article by G.Ward Price entitled 'Why do the Nazis Lie?' in which he criticised the German press – controlled by Goebbels' propaganda ministry – for portraying the Battle of the River Plate as a victory for Germany. In addition Goebbels claimed that the *Graf Spee* had only entered Montevideo harbour 'because the gas-shells used by the British ships had "poisoned the food" on board her, so that she needed reprovisioning'. This drawing was reproduced in the weekly

magazine *The War Illustrated* on 5 January 1940 to accompany an article which revealed that from the beginning of the war until Christmas 1939 no less than 18 German merchant ships had also been scuttled to prevent them falling into Allied hands. It added that 'The scuttling of the *Columbus* [32,581 tons], Germany's third largest liner, off the coast of Virginia on December 19, was the climax of this astounding series of incidents, unique in the history of the sea.'

For his *Daily Mail* work Illingworth usually confined dialogue to the captions of his cartoons. On the few occasions when it appeared inside the drawings themselves he rarely used speech balloons but preferred handwritten text (usually in bold capitals or neat seriffed upper and lower case) set near the speaker's head, as shown here.

1940

THE PHONEY WAR CAME to an abrupt end in April 1940 when Germany invaded Denmark and Norway. The following month attacks came on the Netherlands, Belgium and France which were defenceless against the new kind of rapid mechanised warfare involving tanks and close air support called *Blitzkrieg* (or 'lightning war'). Miraculously, in a successful rearguard action, 200,000 British and 140,000 French troops managed to escape to Britain from the French port of Dunquerque (Dunkirk) after being rescued by hundreds of little boats of every description that had been sent out from the English coast. However, by the end of June the famous French Maginot Line of supposedly impregnable defenceworks had been circumvented by the Germans and France itself had fallen. Hitler was free to impose his so-called 'New Order' on the mainland of Europe, and Britain – now led by its new Prime Minister Winston Churchill – faced the power of the Nazis alone. However, all was not lost and in the summer of 1940 the RAF's defeat of the German Air Force (the Luftwaffe), in what became known as the Battle of Britain, together with successes against Germany's new ally, Italy (which had entered the war in June), gave some reason for hope – despite the horrors of the bombardment of London and other big cities in what became known as the Blitz.

'Only three cartridges – the rest are good-will messages'
Daily Mail, 17 February 1940

Stalin's invasion of the USSR's neighbour, Finland, was not as successful as Hitler's *Blitzkrieg*. After the initial attack on 30 November 1939, the Finns rallied under Marshal Carl von Mannerheim and fought back doggedly. Fearing reprisals from the Soviet Union, the Allies (who were not at war with the USSR) could only offer moral support but no military aid. However, the difficulty the mighty Soviets had in conquering such a small nation suggested to Hitler and the Allies alike that Stalin's much-vaunted Red Army was not all it was cracked up to be.

Previous page: **Chapter One,** *Daily Mail*, 1 June 1940

'Yes, dearie, of course we want a little peace!'
Daily Mail, 27 February 1940

It was announced that the USA would send Sumner Welles, President Roosevelt's Under-Secretary of State, to Europe to try and negotiate a peace settlement. However, as the recent successes of Germany and the Soviet Union in Poland and Finland testified, he would arrive too late. Illingworth has Nazi and Soviet vultures picking over the bloody carcasses of Poland and the Baltic states as Sumner Welles, portrayed as a dove of peace (complete with a traditional olive branch under his wing) looks on.

The Customer is Right Again
Daily Mail, 13 March 1940

After three months of heroic struggle against much larger forces, Finland eventually signed a peace treaty with the Soviet Union. In Illingworth's drawing Foreign Minister Ribbentrop is the wine waiter reporting to a concerned Hitler, proprietor of the Axis Restaurant, that a bottle of 'Axis' champagne opened to celebrate the victory over Finland has been refused by Mussolini. (Italy was still officially neutral at this stage and did not declare war on France and Britain until June 1940.) Chef Joseph Stalin (seen burning the customers' meal on the stove behind), grins as he hears the news.

This is only the second time that Mussolini appears in Illingworth's cartoons (his first was in the *Daily Mail* on 5 February 1940). Up to the end of 1941 Mussolini was, after Hitler, the most caricatured figure by Illingworth on either side of the conflict and by the end of the war was the third (after Hitler and Churchill) most featured of all the war leaders drawn by him.

Winston Destry Rides Again
Daily Mail, 6 April 1940

This drawing comments on Winston Churchill's popular appointment as chairman of the Ministerial Cabinet Defence Committee on 3 April 1940 (Churchill promised a more vigorous prosecution of the war). In this Wild West scene, Churchill (wearing the badge of a newly appointed sheriff and heavily armed) loads his shotgun outside the Allied Courthouse while Prime Minister Chamberlain (who has no weapons at all) takes his hat off to him and holds the spirited horse which is raring to go. The criminals 'Wanted for Murder' are Hitler ('The Blitzkrieg Kid'), Goering ('Hot-Head Hermann') and Goebbels ('Gob' – also a slang word for 'mouth', alluding to his

role as Nazi propaganda minister). In the 1939 film *Destry Rides Again*, James Stewart is the sheriff Destry who tames a rowdy town without violence.

The original of this cartoon is owned by Nicholas Garland OBE, political cartoonist of the *Daily Telegraph* who said of it in 1992: 'I usually have this drawing up in my office and I marvel every day at the way he has drawn Churchill's and Chamberlain's hands. It is quite a good test of a cartoonist's skill; to check whether or not he or she can draw convincing hands. You don't need to do the test on Illingworth, but it is a pleasure to take a close look all the same.'

The Starter's Pistol?
Daily Mail, 10 April 1940

The Phoney War came to a sudden end when German troops marched into Denmark and Norway in the early morning of 9 April 1940. Within 24 hours the Danish had surrendered. Illingworth's cartoon shows Mars, the Roman God of War, dressed in classical armour with a battle helmet and sword. However, in place of the traditional spear he is shown firing a modern starting pistol as he looks at his equally modern stopwatch. In the foreground the combined forces of Britain and France (left) face the German defence lines (right) on the Western Front as barrage balloons fill the sky. Note that the pistol has been discharged on Scandinavia before the main battle has begun.

The Bus
Daily Mail, 7 May 1940

US President Roosevelt and British Prime Minister Neville Chamberlain were the first two wartime leaders to be drawn by Illingworth (both appeared in cartoons in *Punch* in 1937). This is one of the relatively small number (less than a dozen) featuring Chamberlain which Illingworth drew for the *Daily Mail*. It alludes to a speech Chamberlain made to a Conservative Party meeting on 5 April 1940, only days before Germany invaded Denmark and Norway. He said that 'One thing is certain. Hitler has missed the bus.' Events soon proved otherwise and Chamberlain resigned on 10 May, to be succeeded by Winston Churchill.

In Illingworth's drawing, Hitler and Goering, chauffeur-driven in a powerful modern car, overtake the ancient horse-driven London omnibus (bound for Victoria Station – 'Victory-a') with a sleepy Chamberlain at the reins. Public Opinion pokes him with her umbrella and tells him to wake up and various cabinet ministers join the harangue as Churchill waits patiently on the lower deck. (Namsos and Andalsnes were the scenes of unsuccessful Anglo-French landings in Norway.)

***The Ex-Kaiser:* 'Again!'**
Daily Mail, 11 May 1940

On 10 May 1940 German troops invaded the Low
Countries. Within a short time they had overrun
Doorn, near Utrecht in Holland, home since 1919
of the exiled Kaiser Wilhelm II, Germany's leader
during the First World War (who would die the
following year). The Kaiser appears again in
Illingworth's cartoon 'Ghosts' (9 August 1943).

Nearer
Daily Mail, 16 May 1940

After the key defensive Dutch port of Rotterdam was bombed heavily by the Germans Holland surrendered on 14 May. Meanwhile, German panzer divisions broke through into France and Belgium and it only seemed a matter of time before they too suffered the same fate as Poland, Scandinavia and Holland.

In this drawing (captioned 'Heil America!' in the original), Hitler holds up his arm in the Nazi salute as if in reply to the anxious-looking Statue of Liberty holding aloft the flame of freedom in the neutral USA. Beneath Hitler's feet lie the corpses of the conquered nations, Holland uppermost.

Weygand Yesterday: 'I am full of confidence...provided that everyone does his duty with ferocious determination'
Daily Mail, 23 May 1940

On 20 May Paul Reynaud, the French prime minister, appointed the 73-year-old General Maxime Weygand (who had served as Marshal Foch's chief of staff in the First World War) as supreme allied commander. Seen by many as – like Foch and Joan of Arc – the saviour of France, his stirring speeches gave hope to the embattled Allied forces and general public alike. But, despite his attempt to create a new front south of the River Somme known as the Weygand Line, this hope was to prove short-lived.

Reynaud was never drawn by Illingworth during the war and this is the only cartoon to feature the supreme allied commander (note that he is so unfamiliar to British readers that Illingworth has felt it necessary to label him).

The British Game-Cock
Daily Mail, 27 May 1940

Only days after the invasion of the Low Countries, Nazi forces raced through the weakly
defended Ardennes forest area of Belgium and into France. Soon they were forcing
Allied troops back to the Channel coast and German aircraft began to attack RAF
airfields in the south of England. However, they met with stiff resistance.

In Illingworth's cartoon Goering, head of the Luftwaffe, looks on amazed as the
small but plucky British game-cock (complete with RAF roundels on its wings) batters
the much larger Nazi vulture. This is a good example of Illingworth's inability to come
up with 'snappy captions' (see page 25). There are no less than three additional
alternative captions written in pencil on the original drawing. These are: 'The Good
Plucked 'Un' (the original one), 'The Well Plucked One' and 'The English Game Cock'.

Daily Mail, 29 May 1940

There was considerable bewilderment and condemnation when King Leopold III of Belgium surrendered to the Germans on 28 May after only 18 days of fighting, leaving the Allies in a perilous situation. Illingworth's drawing appeared to the left of the headline 'One Man Deserts a Nation' introducing an article by Emrys Jones. It started: 'The Belgian dynasty began with a hero and ends with a weakling. For who can doubt that this line of kings finishes with the ignoble capitulation of Leopold III of the Belgians?'

Illingworth's drawing is a pastiche of Bernard Partridge's famous 1914 *Punch* cartoon about the behaviour of the valiant Albert I, King of the Belgians during the First World War. In the original drawing, entitled 'Unconquerable' (and reproduced next to Illingworth's in the *Daily Mail*), the Kaiser said to Albert: 'So you see you've lost everything.' Albert replied, holding his sword, 'Not my soul'. In Illingworth's drawing Leopold willingly hands his sword over to Hitler. There is a double compliment in Illingworth's cartoon when one is aware that Partridge (known familiarly as B.P.), though by 1940 elderly and frail, was still officially the main political cartoonist on *Punch* until his death in 1945 (when he was succeeded by E.H.Shepard and later, in 1949, by Illingworth himself).

***Napoleon:* 'That's as far as I got, Adolf'**
Daily Mail, 30 May 1940

This cartoon features the ghost of Napoleon behind Hitler, who stands in a Napoleonic pose, with his right hand in his jacket, on piles of bodies in the ruins of a French town and looking out over the English Channel. It comments on the evacuation of British and French troops at Dunkirk on the French coast.

The drawing accompanied an article in the *Daily Mail* about 'fortress Britain' in the early 1800s which began: 'The idea of Britain as a fortress is nothing new. When Napoleon scowled at us across the Channel from Boulogne we hastily built a chain of Martello towers mounted with ordnance to repel invasion…At that time Napoleon was as great a bogy as Hitler is today. In some ways the parallel is extraordinarily exact.' The cartoon was later republished (with its caption translated into Portuguese) as one of a series of postcards produced by the British Embassy in Lisbon, Portugal, and distributed throughout Europe.

'Welcome, Brother!'
Daily Mail, 12 June 1940

Italy declared war on the Allies on 10 June 1940. Many saw the decision of Benito Mussolini to enter the war at this stage as cynical opportunism and in *Punch* magazine on 19 June Illingworth drew Italy's fascist dictator as a scavenging hyena prowling a battlefield strewn with dead bodies.

In this earlier *Daily Mail* drawing Mussolini is seen giving the fascist salute as he ascends the steps of a classical 'Hall of Infamy'. Already there to welcome him are monstrous figures from the past (left to right): Spanish Inquisition torturer Torquemada, Genghis Khan, Roman emperors Caligula and Nero, Cesare and Lucrezia Borgia and Attila the Hun.

As Paris itself faced the threat of the German invaders the French Army fought on bravely, encouraged by the stirring words of the country's prime minister, Paul Reynaud in a midnight radio broadcast to his people on 13 June. Nonetheless, to avoid major bombardment and destruction, the capital was declared an open city by its military governor, General Hering, and on 14 June German troops marched in.

Illingworth has a grim giant goddess representing Paris, sword in hand, and defending her children labelled 'Culture' and 'Art' as the French capital burns (note the Eiffel Tower and Arc de Triomphe in the background).

'We will fight before Paris, we will fight behind Paris' – *M. Reynaud*
Daily Mail, 14 June 1940

A Trump to Beat His Ace?
Daily Mail, 17 June 1940

After the fall of Paris, the situation in France looked desperate. The French government moved to Bordeaux and on 10 June Reynaud sent a telegram to Roosevelt appealing for help. On the 13th the US President replied. As Churchill later noted (*The Second World War*, 1949), Roosevelt's message contained two points which were 'tantamount to belligerence: first, a promise of all material aid, which implied active assistance; secondly, a call to go on fighting even if the government were driven right out of France'. Reynaud saw this as a pledge of help and urged Roosevelt to publish the message. However, his hopes were dashed when the president replied that he could not do so. On 17 June, the day this hopeful cartoon was published, Pétain asked Hitler for an armistice.

Illingworth has Hitler playing cards with Marianne, the national symbol of France (note the revolutionary *bonnet rouge*). Unlike Britannia, Germania, Italia and other female national deities – who had been replaced by Churchill, Hitler, Mussolini *et al.*, Marianne continued to represent France in cartoons throughout the war. This was because – for most cartoonists' – no single powerful individual was seen to represent France. Indeed, with the country divided into Vichy and German-occupied territories from 1940 onwards, France was seen as suffering from a sort of national schizophrenia during most of the conflict. Hence the continued power of Marianne as a symbol.

***John Bull:* 'Maybe, but it should hurt you more than it hurts me'**
Daily Mail, 8 July 1940

After the fall of France, Britain and its empire stood alone against the Axis powers. On 18 June Churchill declared: 'Let us...brave ourselves to our duties, and so bear ourselves that if the British Empire and its Commonwealth last for a thousand years, men will still say: "This was their finest hour".'

This cartoon expresses the determined spirit of the British. As the dentist Hitler invites the next patient to come in to have his teeth extracted (note the hats of the previous countries Germany has conquered), John Bull rolls up his sleeves and produces his own set of pliers to imply that he will not go without a fight.

The Carve-Up
Daily Mail, 26 July 1940

After losing Bessarabia to the Soviet Union and
under pressure from Germany – which had its
eye on the country's oil resources – Romania
agreed to revert to its pre-1912 borders and
ceded two provinces bordering the Black Sea to
Bulgaria. It was later forced to give Transylvania
to Hungary.

    Illingworth's cartoon has Hitler carving up a
trussed King Carol II of Romania for the two little
boys, Hungary and Bulgaria, while Mussolini and
(at the door) Stalin look on.

After Dunkirk the Luftwaffe made an all-out attack on Britain's air defences in what became known as the Battle of Britain. Goering had intended to sweep the RAF from the sky in preparation for a German invasion and the Nazis had even named 13 August 1940 as *Adlertag* – Eagle Day – to accomplish this. However, despite massive raids by Nazi forces the RAF's Fighter Command prevailed. On 20 August Churchill famously declared: 'Never in the field of human conflict was so much owed by so many to so few.'

Illingworth has an RAF Spitfire shooting holes in Goering, depicted as a barrage balloon or 'blimp'. A sad-looking Hitler blimp floats behind.

Letting Out the Hot Air
Daily Mail, 19 August 1940

'Tell me, Heinrich, what <u>does</u> a military objective look like?'
Daily Mail, 28 August 1940

At the end of August 1940 Goering's Luftwaffe changed tactics and switched from attacking the RAF's fighter bases and airfields to night-time bombing raids on British towns and cities.

Illingworth's cartoon comments on the effectiveness of the blackout while also criticising such indiscriminate attacks on non-military targets. This has been drawn on scraperboard, a medium whose use Illingworth pioneered in cartoon art. However, he preferred to employ it for his *Punch* work and this is one of very few scraperboard drawings that Illingworth produced for the *Daily Mail*.

**'What do you mean "When am I going to start the New Order in Europe?"
This IS the New Order'**
Daily Mail, 3 September 1940

As Europe lay in ruins after Nazi invasions and Allied counterattacks by RAF Bomber Command, many civilians in occupied countries expressed concerns about how it was all going to end. Hitler had promised a bright future – a utopian New Order in Europe, with himself as leader of a German master-race, that would be a great improvement on what had gone before. Already, a year after the war had begun, many had their doubts.

In Illingworth's drawing Goering (right) and a German soldier hold the two back legs of Hitler's throne while the front legs are supported by piles of civilian corpses as Europe burns.

'Well, what am I supposed to do now – look frightened?'
Daily Mail, 9 September 1940

On 7 September 1940 Goering began a series of massive bombing raids on London itself in what became knows as the Blitz (short for *Blitzkrieg*). Directing the first daylight attack from a clifftop in France, he sent 350 bombers and 650 fighters across the Channel. Further raids continued on the capital and other cities, day and night, throughout the war.

Illingworth has the figure of Father Thames standing defiant against a spectral Goering caught in the searchlights above recognisable London landmarks such as St Bride's Church in Fleet Street (the church of the British Press, which would later be destroyed by bombing) and St Paul's Cathedral (right). Two days after this cartoon appeared David Low in the *Evening Standard* published a similarly bloated Goering flying through the night sky and dropping bombs on the 'cockney heart' ('Impregnable Target', 11 September 1940).

May the Many Owe Much to <u>These</u> Few
Daily Mail, 4 October 1940

With the resignation of Neville Chamberlain on health grounds, Winston Churchill became prime minister of a new coalition government. His new War Cabinet, portrayed by Illingworth as RAF aircrew next to a bomber piloted by Churchill, included (left to right): Clement Attlee, Arthur Greenwood, Lord Halifax, Lord Beaverbrook, Sir John Anderson, Ernest Bevin and Sir Kingsley Wood.

Daily Mail, 24 October 1940

When the Germans defeated France the new government of Marshal Philippe Pétain sought peace not alliance. As a result France was divided into two parts, the north occupied by Germany and the south, with a new capital at Vichy, run by the French themselves. However, on 22 October 1940, after a number of diplomatic moves, the deputy prime minister of France, Pierre Laval, met Hitler and agreed on collaboration by the Vichy regime, making it an ally of Germany.

Illingworth compares Laval with Judas Iscariot, the disciple who betrayed Jesus for 30 pieces of silver, and shows him selling the soul of France to Hitler. (Note the manacles on the Frenchwoman and the bottle of Vichy water for which the spa town is famous.) Illingworth refused to caricature women in his cartoons and, if at all, tended to draw them very realistically (as in his glamour illustrations for the wartime *Pett's Annual*, 1944).

Much to the annoyance of Hitler – who also thought it a strategic mistake – Mussolini invaded neutral Greece from occupied Albania on 28 October 1940, believing he could expect little resistance from the pro-German Greek dictator General Metaxas.

Albania had been invaded by Italy in April 1939 and this cartoon shows a huge Mussolini marching across the Albanian border into Greece. It appeared alongside a leader which ran: 'Greece joins the long list of small nations who have been knifed in the night [...] just one more victim of the three-o'clock-in-the-morning stroke which has been launched so often and so successfully.'

It's Just Greek to Him
Daily Mail, 29 October 1940

The March on Albania – 1940
Daily Mail, 18 November 1940

In his invasion of Greece Mussolini had not counted on the Greeks' national pride. General Metaxas rejected the Italian ultimatum and the Greek Army fought back valiantly. Less than two weeks after crossing the border, the Italians were in full retreat and by 21 November Greek troops marched in triumph through the streets of the main Italian base in the Albanian town of Koritsa.

Illingworth draws Mussolini as a defeated Napoleon seated backwards on his horse as his troops are driven back through occupied Albania towards the Adriatic coast. This and the previous drawing were reproduced (along with five other *Daily Mail* cartoons by Illingworth, and one *Punch* drawing) in the wartime collection *Salute to Greece: An Anthology of Cartoons Published in the British Press* by S.-L.Hourmouzios (1942).

Taking advantage of Mussolini's retreat through Albania, the British under General Wavell launched their first major land offensive against the Italians in the Western Desert in North Africa. Taking the enemy completely by surprise, more than 35,000 Italian troops were taken prisoner of war in two days, and General Graziani's forces were pushed out of Egypt and into Libya. This cartoon, which appeared without a title when it was originally published in the *Daily Mail*, was reprinted in *400 Famous Cartoons* (1944) with the title 'The Lion's Share!'

'Half is yours if you skin it for me'
Daily Mail, 11 December 1940

St George 1940
Daily Mail, 14 December 1940

The defeat of the Italians in North Africa was reported by Churchill to the House of Commons as a victory of the first order. The *Daily Mail*'s leader-writer, in an editorial set beside this cartoon, saw it as the second of 'two great turning points for the British Empire' since the beginning of the war (the other being the RAF's success in the Battle of Britain in September). In this, the first of a number of cartoons by Illingworth featuring St George (the patron saint of England) and the dragon, Mussolini has already received a major blow to his neck while the monster's other head, Hitler, continues to breathe fiery defiance. Rather muddily printed when it first appeared in the *Daily Mail*, this version reveals the detail of the original drawing.

1941

OR BRITAIN AND ITS ALLIES 1941 was a difficult year. German troops marched into Greece and eventually drove the Allies off the mainland of Europe. In North Africa things also looked grim – to support the retreating Italians Germany sent in Rommel's Afrika Korps who pushed the Allies back as far east as Alexandria in Egypt. At sea Hitler's submarine force (known as *Unterseeboote* or U-boats) accounted for the loss of more than 1200 ships in the Atlantic and a new campaign against his former ally, the Soviet Union, was at first extremely successful. However, early in the year there were signs of hope when the USA agreed to increase military aid to the Allies. Then when the Japanese attacked the American Pacific Fleet at Pearl Harbor, Hawaii, the USA declared war on Japan. In consequence Germany then declared war on the USA and a true world war began.

On 11 March 1941 President Roosevelt signed the Lend-Lease Bill which had been passed by the US Senate and the House of Representatives. By this the USA became 'an arsenal for the democracies' which would send ships, aeroplanes, tanks and guns to the beleaguered Allies on a loan basis. Most of the material would go to Britain but some would also be sent to Greece and China.

Illingworth has (left to right) Ribbentrop, Hitler, Goebbels and Goering relaxing in a 'New Order Picnic' as Roosevelt opens the flood-gates.

Previous page: Daily Mail, 15 April 1941

Opening the Flood-Gates
Daily Mail, 10 March 1941

The Sleep Disturber
Daily Mail, 14 March 1941

The Luftwaffe began a new night-bombing offensive against Britain's cities on 8 March 1941 when London was attacked and Buckingham Palace was hit (despite this King George VI only appears once in cartoons by Illingworth throughout the war – on 3 January 1940 in *Punch*). Raids later followed on Portsmouth, Birmingham, Merseyside, Clydeside, Cardiff, Bristol and Plymouth. However, the government was optimistic that its improved anti-aircraft and night-fighter defences would prove a match for the Luftwaffe, and eight German aircraft were shot down in raids over London on 10 March 1941.

Illingworth draws Luftwaffe chief Hermann Goering as a night-bomber black alley cat – complete with swastika collar tag – being chased off by a well-directed boot labelled 'New AA [Anti-Aircraft] Defences'. The stars he sees read 'Eight down', 'Nine down' and 'Three down' (note the firewatcher using a stirrup-pump to douse the cat with water).

The Panzer's Tail
Daily Mail, 18 April 1941

This powerful image by Illingworth has the British bulldog (wearing a Royal Navy cap) standing in the Mediterranean near Italy and biting the tail of the German panzer/panther robot (note the tank tracks on its rear feet) in Libya. This alludes to the newly arrived German Afrika Korps' battle with the Allies in North Africa and the successful harassing of Rommel's supply line from Sicily by Royal Navy ships based in Malta. A notable incident took place on 16 April when the Royal Navy sank five German supply ships and their escort of three destroyers en route between Sicily and the Libyan seaport of Tripoli.

Hurry Up With the Armour for St George!
Daily Mail, 23 April 1941

As German troops marched into Greece and Rommel's forces crossed the Egyptian border from Libya many Allied leaders complained of the quality of British tanks against Germany's superior panzers and anti-tank weapons. However, the government promised that newly reorganised armoured divisions – incorporating Cruiser tanks, motorised infantry and anti-aircraft and anti-tank guns – would soon be in action.

Published on St George's Day, Illingworth's cartoon has the Royal Navy bulldog and RAF seagull doing their best to contain the giant Hitler dragon while Churchill, as St George, straps on his new armour. The same day Illingworth produced a similar cartoon for *Punch* with a medieval knight in armour facing a huge Nazi dragon in an allusion to Christian's encounter with Apollyon in Chapter IX of John Bunyan's *The Pilgrim's Progress* (1678).

Sting-time
Daily Mail, 16 June 1941

Wartime shortages meant that petrol and many foodstuffs were rationed, paid for by coupons which were strictly allocated. On 1 June 1941 this went further and rationing was introduced on clothing, followed by coal in July. However there was a flourishing black market selling at inflated prices for those who were willing to pay – fish, in particular, being sold for enormous profits.

This is one of the first major solo appearances in the *Daily Mail* of Illingworth's character John Citizen (prototypes for whom appeared in *Punch* on 22 February 1939 and the *Daily Mail* on 8 December 1939). In this drawing he is shown being besieged by profiteers in the form of summertime stinging insects as he toils in the fields. 'John Citizen', originally created by 'Poy' – Illingworth's predecessor at the *Daily Mail* –

was an Everyman, 'Joe Bloggs' figure, a sort of modern John Bull. A long-suffering middle-class character, in Illingworth's wartime version he is usually depicted as a middle-aged man, too old for wartime service, left at home during the conflict but who does his best for the war effort by working in factories and on an allotment growing food. He is always depicted as clean-shaven, but sports a small moustache, has short hair, and wears a trilby hat and mackintosh or working overalls with rolled-up sleeves. Fit-looking (and only rarely wearing glasses) and not at all comical (unlike Strube's 'Little Man' figure in the *Daily Express*), it is assumed that he is a father or genial uncle figure with a son or nephew at the war (yet he rarely appears with a family or wife).

On 22 June 1941, at 3.15 in the morning, Germany launched Operation Barbarossa and invaded the Soviet Union along an 1800-mile front from the Baltic to the Black Sea. This was a direct breach of the Nazi-Soviet Pact signed in 1939 and took Stalin – and the world – completely by surprise. Three million troops supported by more than 3000 tanks, 7000 guns and almost 3000 aircraft rapidly swept across the USSR.

Illingworth portrays this as literally a stab in the back for Stalin who is so shocked that he drops his pipe and the Russo-German Pact. The *Daily Mail* leader beside the cartoon read: 'A mildly astonished world awoke yesterday to find Hitler's legions marching across the frontiers of Russia. Immediate reactions were many, varied and mostly emotional. [...] Nemesis is threatened for the wily Stalin. He is paying the penalty now for a policy of brutal cynicism and a series of shattering political blunders.'

'Forgive me, comrade, but it seemed <u>such</u> a good opportunity!'
Daily Mail, 23 June 1941

Dead Weight
Daily Mail, 2 July 1941

As well as rationing of fuel and foodstuffs, the British Government also controlled the flow of daily news through newspapers and radio broadcasts (television was not widely available until the 1950s). The lack of news about the war caused great public irritation. On at least two earlier occasions (29 July and 7 December 1940), the *Daily Mail*'s leader column had openly criticised the government in this matter (both items were accompanied by equally cutting Illingworth cartoons). In the earlier of these, news of the sinking of the troopship *Lancastria* off the French coast on 17 June 1940 – with the loss of nearly 3000

lives – was not announced in Britain until it had first been published in the USA on 24 July, though Germany had broadcast the information the next day.

In Illingworth's cartoon the tiny muzzled donkey being led by an authoritarian Foreign Office figure and weighed down by army and navy service censors has the face of the minister of information, Duff Cooper (who was replaced soon after this drawing was published – see page 26). Behind, and trying to attract attention as the procession approaches across an empty landscape, a messenger tries to deliver the news.

Taxi to Moscow
Daily Mail, 1 September 1941

As Nazi troops raced across the Soviet Union towards Moscow the cost in German lives
mounted at an alarming rate, but still Hitler urged his generals onwards.

The German equivalent of the John Citizen character during the Second World War,
as drawn by British and Allied cartoonists – including Illingworth – tended to be a fat,
elderly burgher (with his blond hair *en brosse*) wearing a Tyrolean hat and lederhosen,
smoking a pipe, drinking from a beerstein, eating sausages and sauerkraut and
accompanied by a dachshund. His wife would usually be depicted wearing a dirndl and
would often have her long blonde hair in plaits. Illingworth has a typical German couple
dressed in traditional clothing in a taxicab driven from Germany to Moscow by the
Führer himself. Hitler's eyes stare firmly forward at the road ahead despite the cries
at the human cost of the Russian Campaign by the woman and the sweating man.
To emphasise Hitler's isolation and single-mindedness, a sign above the meter reads:
'To speak to the Führer is forbidden.'

Travelling Companions
Daily Mail, 30 September 1941

Reinhardt Heydrich, who had proved a ruthless and much-feared deputy to Gestapo chief
Heinrich Himmler, was appointed Reich Protector of German-occupied Bohemia and Moravia
(now the Czech Republic) at the end of September 1941. He immediately declared martial law
to subdue all opposition to the Nazi occupation. Hundreds of Czechs were rounded up and
many evicted from their homes to make room for German immigrants from the Baltic States.
Heydrich was murdered in Prague by Czech assassins the following year.

In this, the first of only two wartime drawings Illingworth made of Heydrich, the figures
who accompany him to Prague are Hatred and Death (portrayed as a skeleton wearing an
SS officer's uniform).

'*Wunderschön!* I can smell the burning!'
Daily Mail, 24 October 1941

As Hitler's troops approached the outskirts of Moscow RAF bombers began to make large-scale attacks on Hamburg, Stuttgart and other German cities.

Illingworth has Hitler viewing distant Moscow through long-range field glasses across a battlefield strewn with corpses but mistakes the burning of the Russian capital for the smell of his own greatcoat set on fire by 'RAF raids'. This cartoon was also reprinted on the front page of the London-produced French-language aerial propaganda newspaper *Le Courrier de l'Air* which was dropped by the RAF over occupied France. The text of the cartoon was translated into French and relettered.

Justice!
Daily Mail, 25 October 1941

In reprisal for the killing of Lieutenant-Colonel
Karl Holz, German commander of Nantes in
Vichy-controlled France, 50 French civilians were
shot on 21 October 1941. A similar incident (with
similar consequences) took place in Bordeaux
shortly afterwards. Illingworth has Death in the
guise of a German officer weighing the balance.

Old Adolf Hubbard
Daily Mail, 1 November 1941

This cartoon by Illingworth depicts Hitler as the nursery-rhyme character Old Mother Hubbard with a huge starving Nazi army hound as her 'little doggy'. It alludes to the fact that the Red Army moved their factories eastwards and deliberately employed a 'scorched earth' policy as they retreated before the Germans, leaving nothing in the way of food, equipment or industrial wealth and thus making the Nazi forces totally dependent on their already stretched supply line.

This drawing was later exhibited at the major exhibition 'Drawn and Quartered: The World of the British Newspaper Cartoon, 1720-1970' held at the National Portrait Gallery in London in 1970 and sponsored by the Newspaper Publishers' Association and the British Cartoonists' Association. Other wartime *Daily Mail* cartoons by Illingworth in the exhibition – which was opened by Princess Margaret – included those published on 17 November 1939 (see page 34), 7 May 1940 (see page 43), 4 August 1941, 28 September 1941 and 7 June 1944 (see page 123).

By the end of October the Germans had begun to lay siege to Moscow but were soon bogged down by mud and wet weather. With the beginning of the Russian winter, they were able to move their tanks and heavy armour over the frost-hardened ground and began a fresh major assault on 15 November. However the extreme cold (minus 40 degrees Celsius) now became a serious problem for the Germans whose equipment and troops were not used to such extreme conditions.

Illingworth was a keen skier and had first seen Hitler and other Nazi leaders at close quarters in the 1930s when he had visited Garmisch, the winter sports centre near Munich (see page 18). Some of his earliest cartoons for *Punch* (e.g. 22 January 1936 and 1 November 1937) featured skiing holidays.

The Learner
Daily Mail, 19 November 1941

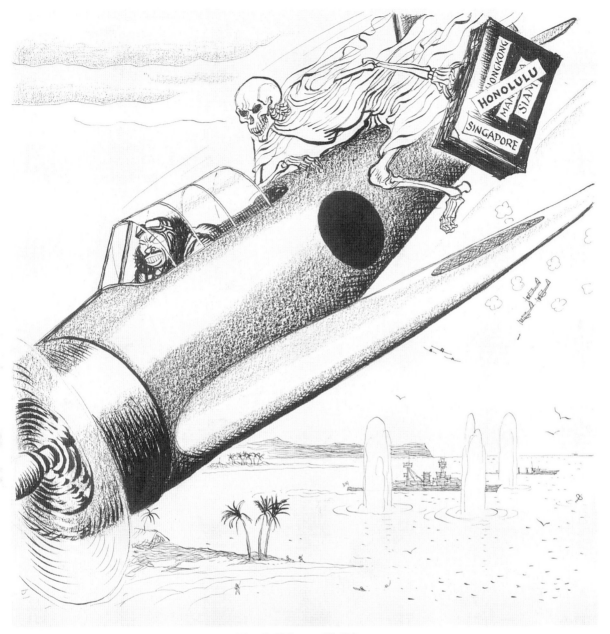

Death Takes a Holiday
Daily Mail, 9 December 1941

On 7 December 1941, Japan and the USA entered the Second World War when 184 Japanese aircraft attacked the US Pacific Fleet in its base at Pearl Harbor in Hawaii, sinking or disabling 19 warships, destroying nearly 200 aircraft and killing more than 2000 Americans.

Illingworth depicts the figure of Death riding on the back of a Japanese torpedo bomber as it attacks Pearl Harbor. The suitcase stickers show recent Japanese successes with Honolulu, the capital of Hawaii, as the topmost. (The film *Death Takes a Holiday*, starring Fredric March, was released in 1934.)

Just Another Milestone
Daily Mail, 31 December 1941

As the third year of war drew to a close the prospects for Hitler's Germany began to look bleak. There was also considerable surprise when Hitler announced on 21 December that, after the failure to take Moscow, he had sacked Field Marshal Walter Von Brauchitsch as Commander-in-Chief of the German Army and had taken personal command of the armed forces himself. The *Daily Mail*'s leader column made much of this, calling it 'the most startling admission of military disaster yet to emerge from Germany. [...] The effect of this on the already uneasy German people can only be devastating.'

Illingworth's cartoon implies that, at the turn of the year, Hitler has lost his way as he personally tries to lead his ragged and disillusioned troops through inclement weather across a bleak and barren landscape (note that his 'war map' has been discarded and is rolled up under his arm).

1942

THE AXIS POWERS OF Germany, Japan and Italy continued to succeed in the early part of 1942 with the Japanese in particular achieving spectacular success in the Philippines, Hong Kong, Burma, Malaya, Singapore, Indonesia and the Pacific, and they had even begun to threaten Australia. However, the American naval victory over the Japanese Fleet at Midway Island, Hawaii, redressed the balance considerably. Also, though in Europe the Nazis had managed to push the Red Army back to Stalingrad in the south and Moscow and Leningrad in the north, before long they found themselves bogged down with the prospect of a long winter ahead. Likewise, by the end of the year the British Eighth Army in North Africa – re-equipped and with new commanders such as Montgomery and Alexander – began to gain ground against the formerly invincible Afrika Korps, and the arrival of US troops from Algeria put pressure on the Axis forces from both sides. The tide had begun to turn for the Allies. As Churchill said in November: 'This is not the end. It is not even the beginning of the end. But it is, perhaps, the end of the beginning.'

As Japanese troops occupied the Philippines Illingworth's cartoon contrasts Japan's spectacular success with Germany's military reverses. Hitler is depicted as a gloomy burnt-out firework falling to earth while a grinning General Tojo of Japan rockets skywards, the sparks in his wake giving the names of recent victories (HMS *Repulse* and HMS *Prince of Wales* were two British warships sunk off Singapore).

Daily Mail, 2 January 1942

Previous page: **Bushido – the Way of a Warrior,** *Daily Mail,* 11 March 1942

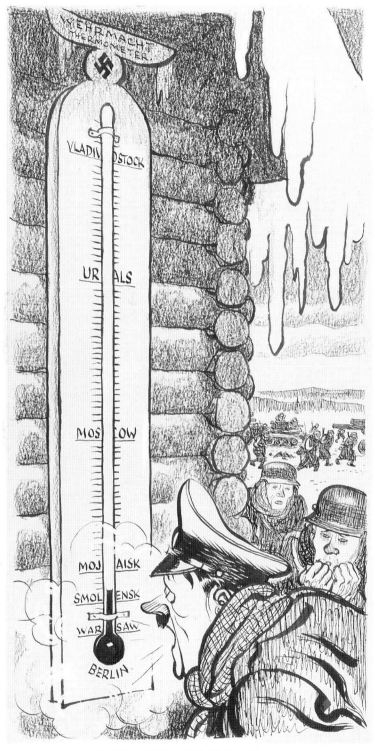

The Soviet counter-offensive on the Eastern Front reached a major turning point with the taking of Mojaisk (Mozhaysk), the German base at the centre of their defensive line, after a siege of six weeks. Opening the road to Smolensk and the great sweep westward towards Poland and Germany itself, it was a key victory. As the *Daily Mail* editorial besides Illingworth's drawing reported: 'This is, without question, the most important Russian victory of the campaign. The last threat to Moscow has been removed, and the last German pretence to be holding a winter line has been blasted into nothing.'

Illingworth shows Hitler – surrounded by frost-bitten troops dressed in inadequate winter clothing and blowing on their hands to keep warm – breathing on the 'Wehrmacht Thermometer' in an attempt to reverse its fall.

No Use, Hitler – It's Going Down
Daily Mail, 22 January 1942

Her Greatest Test
Daily Mail, 24 January 1942

The war began to reach further south when 5000 Japanese troops invaded the islands of New Britain and New Ireland in New Guinea after a carrier-borne aerial assault and raised the Rising Sun flag on Australian territory. Fearing an invasion of Australia itself, Britain's old cricketing adversary – famous for the annual Test Match battles for the Ashes – began to prepare for the worst.

This cartoon (note the Australian digger in the kangaroo's pouch) was later reproduced in the German weekly *Das Reich* in 1942 as part of a special double-page feature attacking the *Daily Mail* which it saw as 'a prism of the English "everyday"'. In an article reporting the fact ('Goebbels Dislikes Us – But He Reads Us', 4 March 1942) Froom Tyler began by remarking that 'It was Bonaparte who discovered that newspapers were more to be feared than bayonets.'

Fun While It Lasts
Daily Mail, 18 February 1942

At the end of the Malayan Campaign – one of the most disastrous in British military history –
a Japanese force under Lieutenant-General Tomoyuki Yamashita captured the island of
Singapore. Avoiding the 50 massive British fortress guns pointing out to sea, the Japanese took
prisoner more than 130,000 British, Australian and Indian troops – plus a huge haul of rifles,
machine-guns and field artillery – for a loss of only 10,000 men.

Illingworth depicts Japanese Commander-in-Chief General Hideki Tojo as a cheeky monkey
dressed up as the governor of Singapore in Australia's bedroom (note the slouch hat on the
bed). A pair of boots labelled 'Java' and 'Sumatra' stand near the bed and the uniforms of India,
New Zealand and Burma can be seen in the wardrobe – implying that all these might be next.

'Look what the cat's brought in!'
Daily Mail, 17 April 1942

After German pressure, Pierre Laval, who had
been dismissed by French premier Marshal
Pétain in December 1940, was reinstated as head
of the Vichy Government. He would also serve as
minister for foreign affairs, the interior and
information. In Illingworth's cartoon, the 'spirit
of France' looks on anxiously as the pro-Nazi
premier, depicted as a cat which Pétain had tried
to drown by tying a brick round its neck, returns
with four odious kittens labelled 'End of US Aid',
'Re-Entry into War', 'Dishonour' and 'Slavery'.

Daily Mail, 23 April 1942

Another version of St George and the dragon, published on St George's Day as rumours
abounded of Allied troops being massed to invade German-occupied Europe from Britain.
In this cartoon – featuring a coin or commemorative medal design – it is an Allied airborne
forces figure who is seen attacking the winged Hitler dragon as warships sail across the
English Channel. This is the original drawing – the version finally printed in the *Daily Mail*
had 'St George's Year?' under the date at the bottom of the coin (the question mark from which
can still be seen).

The Bigwig
Daily Mail, 28 April 1942

In a proclamation read to the German Parliament (or *Reichstag*) Adolf Hitler assumed total power in Germany and abolished all laws that might restrict his will. As well as being leader of the nation, supreme commander of the armed forces, and head of the government, he was now also supreme law lord with absolute power of life and death over every German.

Is Your Journey Really Necessary?
Daily Mail, 23 May 1942

Following a major offensive by the Germans on the Eastern Front to clear the Kerch Peninsula in the Ukraine and thereby open the way to the Caucasus oilfields, Soviet Marshal Timoshenko led a counter-offensive at Kharkov. Meanwhile, the Japanese completed their occupation of Burma.

Illingworth's cartoon is a pastiche of the famous British government wartime poster campaign by various artists. The best known of these, produced for the Railway Executive Committee by Bert Thomas OBE, featured a British soldier standing in front of a railway ticket booth and facing the viewer as he utters these words. In Illingworth's published version

Timoshenko (in his first appearance in cartoons by Illingworth) is the ticket-seller in a booth marked 'Book Here for All Parts of the USSR' who grabs Hitler by the throat. The surprised traveller in the background is Tojo (bound for Burma) who is himself standing beside a spoof of another famous British travel poster, 'Skegness is *so* Bracing' (1908) by John Hassall (Vladivostok is on the east coast of the USSR and thus Hitler's ultimate destination). The original version (shown here) has a British Tommy in the booth instead of Timoshenko, 'The World' replaces 'The USSR' and the label on Hitler's suitcase is 'Exile' instead of 'Caucasus.'

Daily Mail, 1 June 1942

In retaliation for German bombings of civilians in
London, Coventry, Bath and Plymouth (seen here
as ghostly figures along with those from Warsaw,
Belgrade and Rotterdam), the RAF began a series
of colossal 1000-bomber raids against German
cities. The first raid on Cologne was at that time
the most concentrated and destructive night-time
attack in history.

Daily Mail, 29 June 1942

Though the German military machine seemed at
first to be unstoppable, little by little the British
Eighth Army began to slow down Rommel's
troops in North Africa and the Soviet Red Army
started to make progress against Field Marshal
von Bock's Wehrmacht forces in the USSR.

Cutting Out the Frills
Daily Mail, 6 July 1942

Because of wartime shortages of raw materials in Britain, cheap 'utility' clothing and furniture were introduced in 1942 along with the government's 'Make Do and Mend' campaign. As a result of these measures the hemlines on women's dresses rose, pleats and designs using a lot of fabric were limited and men's turn-ups and double-breasted suits became scarce.

After the First World War, the classical national figure of Britannia largely faded away from cartoons. Nevertheless Illingworth still used her occasionally during the Second World War, as here, with Hugh Dalton – minister for economic warfare (1940) and president of the Board of Trade (1942) – trimming her dress. Illingworth also continued to use Britannia occasionally after the war, notably in a cover for *Time* magazine in January 1963 (see page 28).

'Faster! Faster!'
Daily Mail, 13 July 1942

The situation in North Africa changed dramatically when Rommel captured Tobruk taking 35,000 Allied prisoners. Meanwhile, the Germans were also having considerable success on the Eastern Front as Field Marshal Von Bock – aided by heavy reinforcements – thrust forward to the westerly banks of the River Don en route to Stalingrad and the Caucasus oilfields.

The cartoonist has Von Bock (in the second of only two wartime cartoons by Illingworth to feature him) as the stoker shovelling Axis manpower into the firebox of a steam train labelled the 'Caucasus Express' and driven by Hitler. David Low drew a very similar cartoon two months later in the *Evening Standard* ('More!', 4 September 1942).

Daily Mail, 3 August 1942

The German Army successfully crossed the River Don in the Ukraine, obtained footholds in the Caucasus itself and headed for Stalingrad. In its leader column for 27 July the *Daily Mail* wrote: 'The Russian situation is today more dangerous than it has been at any time since Hitler launched his attack last year.'

Illingworth has an ecstatic Hitler on a roller-coaster ride – previous peaks of delight being the Fall of France and the taking of Crete and Greece – while a woman representing the German public hangs on terrified behind him.

Daily Mail, 14 September 1942

The Battle of Stalingrad (now Volgograd) was one of the bloodiest conflicts in the war, with German and Romanian troops fighting the Red Army through the suburbs of the city, building by building. Though their task seemed impossible Soviet troops held on resolutely against massive tank attacks. Eventually, helped by winter snows, the Red Army mounted a counterattack and encircled the German Sixth Army in a pincer movement, cutting it off from its supply line.

'Now, if you're ready, Oysters dear,
  We can begin to feed'
'But not on us!' the Oysters cried,
  Turning a little blue.
'After such kindness, that would be
  A dismal thing to do!'
'The night is fine,' the Walrus said.
  'Do you admire the view?'

The Walrus and the Carpenter
('If anyone has to starve, it will not be the Germans' – *Goering*)
Daily Mail, 5 October 1942

On 4 October 1942, as Germany's position began to look increasingly desperate, Hermann Goering made what the *Daily Mail* described as 'the most remarkable speech to come out of Germany this year'. Amongst the menacing remarks it contained were: 'Whoever starves, it will not be Germany', directed at the conquered territories, and 'We have shot no generals so far...but the shooting of a general is not impossible...all cowards will be treated alike', aimed at the leadership of the Germany Army.

In this pastiche of John Tenniel's illustration from Lewis Carroll's *Through the Looking Glass* (1872), Goering is the Walrus and Hitler the carpenter about to eat oysters with the names of Germany's allies (left to right): Tojo of Japan, Pétain and Laval of France, Quisling of Denmark, Antonescu of Romania, King Boris III of Bulgaria, Mannerheim of Finland, Mussolini, and Admiral Horthy of Hungary.

Of course, I never really meant to kill it.

Second Thoughts
Daily Mail, 10 October 1942

In this powerful image of the battle for Stalingrad, Illingworth draws Hitler as a small cowardly dog with its tail between its legs, scarred on one cheek, with a sore nose and walking away from defeat in a trail of blood. Meanwhile, Stalin is the prickly hedgehog or porcupine rolled into a ball whose bloody spines have caused these injuries.

Wooden Cross Island
Daily Mail, 14 October 1942

As an essential part of the supply route to Allied forces in North Africa, as well as a base
for the RAF to attack Rommel's own supply line, the Mediterranean island of Malta
(then part of the British Empire) received repeated bombing attacks by the Luftwaffe
from 1940 to 1943, with particularly heavy raids taking place in 1942. On 15 April 1942
King George VI awarded the George Cross 'to the Island Fortress of Malta to bear witness
to a heroism and devotion that will long be famous in history'.

The Liberators
Daily Mail, 9 November 1942

While General Montgomery's Eighth Army launched the El Alamein offensive in Egypt, the Allies
also began Operation Torch in French North Africa. Employing formidable Anglo-American
naval, air and land forces, the first landings were made in Morocco and Algeria by US
commandos and airborne troops.

'Now <u>you</u> lead for a change'
Daily Mail, 25 November 1942

As German troops became bogged down around
Stalingrad it began to look as if Hitler's famous
'intuition' which had guided him thus far, often
against the advice of his generals, had finally
begun to fail him.

'At least I <u>took</u> Moscow first'
Daily Mail, 27 November 1942

Partly because it was named after the Soviet leader, Hitler wanted to take Stalingrad at all costs, even before taking the capital, Moscow. By the same token Stalin was determined that it would not be captured and launched a massive counter-attack on 19 November, completely encircling the Germans and cutting them off from their supply line. Illingworth's cartoon alludes to Napoleon's own defeat against the Russians.

Daily Mail, 14 December 1942

On 13 December 1942 the British Jewish community observed a day of mourning for their European brethren persecuted by the Nazis. Later the same week Foreign Secretary Anthony Eden read out in the House of Commons a declaration by Allied governments condemning the extermination of Europe's Jews (especially in Poland) and warning those responsible that they would face retribution after the war. The declaration was broadcast across Europe by the BBC and other Allied radio stations.

1943

AFTER YEARS ON THE DEFENSIVE the Allies finally began to take the attack to the Axis powers in 1943. By the end of the year not only had all Axis forces in North Africa surrendered, but the Allies had also landed on the mainland of Italy, defeated Mussolini and the Italian Army and forced the new Italian government to change sides and declare war on Germany. Meanwhile, in northern Europe the Soviet Red Army had stopped the Nazis in their tracks and had begun to drive them westwards while massive bomber raids from Britain pounded major German cities in an attempt to halt industrial production and break civilian morale. Added to which, the formation of South-East Asia Command (SEAC) had helped co-ordinate Chinese, American and British Empire forces fighting against the Japanese in the jungles of Burma and elsewhere, resulting in considerable successes in this theatre as well. The boot was now firmly on the other foot.

Morning After...
Daily Mail, 1 January 1943

For the first three years of the Second World War, each New Year's Day seemed to mark further successes by Hitler and Germany's Axis partners in Europe. However, on 1 January 1943, after a number of defeats across the Continent, and with a Second Front attack by the Allies imminent, things began to look bleak for the Nazis. Illingworth has Hitler and Goebbels suffering from hangovers after a New Year's Eve champagne banquet while a German boy opens the curtains on the dawn of 1943 and the figure of Death arrives with the bill.

Previous page: Daily Mail, 30 January 1943

ILLINGWORTH'S WAR IN CARTOONS

In a single week the Red Army dealt the Germans a number of major blows over a front more than 1000 miles long, recapturing the key town of Mozdok in the Caucasus as well as Morozovsk, the main Luftwaffe airfield supplying German troops attacking Stalingrad, and driving on through the Russian steppe (treeless plains) country.

Illingworth has Soviet Marshals Timoshenko and Zhukov (his only appearance in Illingworth's wartime cartoons) kicking Hitler down the steps leading away from Victory (note Stalin in the doorway) and towards a frostbitten future as personified by Generals January and February.

Steppe by Steppe
Daily Mail, 5 January 1943

105

Daily Mail, 18 January 1943

After years of determined resistance to the Nazi steamroller, the Soviet Union, with its enormous reserves of manpower and industrial resources began, to retaliate with a vengeance. This cartoon shows an enormous Russian bear (with a hammer and sickle logo on its back), which has tied the barrel of a rifle marked 'Wehrmacht' into a knot, advancing onto a cornered and defenceless Hitler. It was published in the *Daily Mail* shortly after a 2000-gun assault heralded the launching of Operation Iskra to break the German siege of Leningrad. At the same time the Red Army made a ferocious attack on Axis forces south of Voronezh, 300 miles north-west of Stalingrad on the Upper Don River, in which the Hungarian Second Army was crushed.

This drawing is a good example of the use of size to lampoon opponents, a principle that has been commented on by Sigmund Freud in *Jokes and Their Relation to the Unconscious* (1905): 'Caricature, parody and travesty are directed against people and objects which lay claim to authority and respect, who are in some sense exalted...By making our enemy small, inferior, despicable or comic we achieve in a roundabout way the enjoyment of overcoming him – to which a third person bears witness by his laughter.'

After massive Soviet assaults on the German Sixth Army attacking Stalingrad – by now cut off, encircled and only supplied by air – the inevitable result seemed to be only a matter of time. Two days after this cartoon was published Field Marshal Friedrich von Paulus, commander-in-chief of the Sixth Army, surrendered. According to Russian sources 120,000 Germans were killed in the battle for Stalingrad and more than 90,000 (including 24 generals) were taken prisoner.

A French version of this cartoon was later reproduced in *Le Courrier de l'Air Illustré* a special supplement to *Le Courrier de l'Air*, a London-produced aerial propaganda newspaper which was dropped by the RAF over occupied France. (See also page 26).

'As promised, *mein Führer*, we have raised the swastika over Stalingrad'
Daily Mail, 29 January 1943

The Hitler Mystery: A Few Solutions
Daily Mail, 15 March 1943

There were rumours of another assassination attempt on Hitler and much speculation that something had happened to him, fuelled by the fact that, for a while, most radio broadcasts were given by propaganda minister Joseph Goebbels. However, Hitler was unharmed – the bomb planted on the plane carrying him from a military conference in Smolensk to his headquarters in Rastenburg on 13 March had failed to detonate.

In this multi-frame cartoon (unusual for Illingworth) the artist speculates on where Hitler is – dead, working as a painter, with his former deputy Rudolf Hess (his only appearance in a cartoon by Illingworth) who had flown to Britain in 1941, ill from biting the edge of carpets (a curious psychological condition he had), in disguise, or hiding in his mountain retreat at Berchtesgaden (misspelt on this original but corrected when published) in Bavaria.

Daily Mail, 29 March 1943

To celebrate the 25th anniversary of the founding of the RAF, Illingworth has drawn a Nazi birthday
cake with 25 candles, each of which represents a German city being set alight by the British. The *Daily
Mail* published an article to accompany this cartoon which reminded readers that the newspaper had
offered a number of prizes for pioneer aviators. Winners included A.V.Roe (1907 – later to create the
Lancaster bomber), RAF officers Alcock and Brown (1919, the first flight across the Atlantic) and Amy
Johnson (1930, first solo flight to Australia). Added to which, its proprietor Lord Rothermere had even
funded the research for the plane that would become the famous Bristol Blenheim bomber.

The Lie-Phoon
Daily Mail, 30 April 1943

In this unusual anthropomorphic image, Illingworth has transformed Nazi propaganda minister Joseph Goebbels into a 'lying' version of the successful 400mph British fighter, the Hawker Typhoon. The 'Lie-Phoon' – complete with Goebbels' trademark spats – is being admired on the runway by Hitler and Luftwaffe chief Goering. The published version omits the words 'sneer', 'praise', 'help' and 'lie'.

This cartoon was undoubtedly also inspired by a public statement made at this time by Joseph Goebbels: 'British caricatures of German types are insulting, because they are no longer truthful. The National Socialists have completely transformed the German people.' On 26 April 1943 Vicky (Victor Weisz, 1913-66), also drew a cartoon ('All My Own Work') for the *News Chronicle* lampooning the statement and showing Goebbels painting a portrait of the Nazi leaders as angelic figures.

Daily Mail, 13 May 1943

This cartoon, untitled when originally published but later sometimes captioned 'A Fair Cop', has Hitler as a cat-burglar trapped in a window by Stalin as he tries to escape (note that his ladder has fallen down) and looking anxiously at policemen Churchill and Roosevelt with truncheons labelled 'Second Front'. The drawing was published on the day when the Allies triumphed over Rommel in North Africa, capturing 250,000 troops, and intensive bombings of Sardinia led Axis leaders to think (mistakenly) that the Second Front would take place there in the near future. Illingworth returned to this theme in 'The Long Drop' (22 June 1944) with Finland caught on Stalin's window-ledge and Hitler running away with the ladder (labelled 'German Support') as Churchill and Roosevelt, again as policemen, chase after him.

Daily Mail, 17 May 1943

In this unusual double drawing, Illingworth reworks his own *Daily Mail* cartoon from 1 May 1940 showing Hitler astride the Nazi winged beast setting fire to Poland and facing the guns of Holland, France, Belgium and Britain. The new image has a giant winged RAF figure setting 'German Industries' ablaze in the Battle of the Ruhr as Hitler and Mussolini run away. This cartoon was published on the day that news broke of the successful breaching of a number of hydroelectric dams in the Ruhr district by 'Dambuster' squadrons of RAF Lancasters using special 'bouncing bombs'.

The giant gas-mask-wearing winged German monster man, crawling over a tiny Europe and destroying as it goes, is probably the most powerful of the Nazi chimerae created by Illingworth. It first appeared in the double-page colour cartoon 'The Combat' (*Punch Almanack*, 6 November 1939), facing a tiny Allied plane labelled 'Freedom' and with a British roundel on one wing and a French one on the other.

Hard Pounding This, Gentlemen!
Daily Mail, 26 May 1943

Another powerful image of the British bombing raids on German factories, this time a
giant RAF officer uses a 4000lb bomb to grind industrial sites like a pestle and mortar.
On the night of 23-24 May, RAF aircraft dropped 2000 tons of bombs on Dortmund
alone. Meanwhile, Allied air forces also attacked airfields in Italy, Sicily and Sardinia in
an attempt to neutralise the German and Italian air forces. Mussolini sweats as, trapped
in a retort, he is heated by a British Bunsen gas burner.

113

Daily Mail, 7 June 1943

On 31 May USAAF Flying Fortress bombers attacked Naples. After the Mediterranean island of Pantelleria near Sicily was shelled heavily on the same day by a British cruiser and two destroyers, fears of an imminent Allied invasion in the south of Italy drove thousands of Italians northwards.

Illingworth has the British lion, having just eaten the Afrika Korps, attacking Mussolini (dressed as a Roman Emperor and holding a bent sword labelled 'German Help') in his box at the Colosseum in Ancient Rome. Meanwhile, Hitler (left) and a German Army officer run away.

An Experiment Well Worth Trying
Daily Mail, 25 June 1943

Using ever more powerful high-explosive and incendiary bombs and new radar-guided 'Pathfinder' aircraft to improve the accuracy of attacks, the RAF made huge air-raids on Germany's industrial cities such as Essen (home of the Krupp armaments works) and Düsseldorf. In Britain a 'Wings for Victory' National Savings campaign was also begun to collect money to build still more bombers.

This cartoon appeared opposite an editorial defending the massive destruction resulting from the Allied 'air terror' particularly on Düsseldorf, many pictures of which had been published in Britain. As the *Daily Mail* said: 'This is not damage but devastation. [...] We may recognise the appalling power of this weapon without abating one jot of our determination to use it to the full against our enemies. [...] It is as if the Allies, to save the lives of their soldiers, are reaching out with a huge mechanical arm to crush and demoralise the enemy.' Illingworth has Air Vice-Marshal Sir Arthur Harris, head of Bomber Command, turning the heat on Hitler and Mussolini to extract the spirit of defeat.

– And Now the Chatter Bug
Daily Mail, 11 August 1943

The Squander Bug (originally 'The Money Grub') was a cartoon character created by the poster artist
Philip Boydell for the National Savings Committee and was used as a propaganda tool by the British
government to warn consumers about wastage on the Home Front. In later versions the hairs on its body
were replaced by swastikas and it was drawn by many cartoonists. Illingworth has created a variation in
the form of the 'Chatter Bug' to warn the public – personified here as John Citizen, working in a
munitions factory on the 'war job' – about listening to overly optimistic gossip about an Allied victory at
a time when the war could still go either way.

Mein Cramp
Daily Mail, 19 August 1943

Hitler's dreams of world domination began to fade as Allied successes mounted in the autumn of 1943. In this cartoon, Hitler – dressed as a Teutonic warrior and armed only with a sword and an ever-shrinking Luftwaffe shield – is surrounded by lances from the countries that will soon be liberated by the Allies and which before long will be fighting back. (Monty is General Montgomery, head of the British Eighth Army, who defeated Rommel in North Africa in 1942 and played an important part in the subsequent invasion of Sicily and Italy.) The title 'Mein Cramp' is an allusion to Hitler's famous pre-war autobiographical book, *Mein Kampf* (My Struggle).

RAF bombers made three saturation raids on Berlin in 11 nights, on one occasion dropping 1000 tons of bombs in just 20 minutes. Meanwhile, at the Quadrant Conference in Quebec, Churchill, Roosevelt and Canadian Prime Minister Mackenzie King agreed to a Second Front against Germany from France to be codenamed Operation Overlord. Illingworth shows Stalin and Soviet Foreign Affairs Commissar Viachislav Molotov (in one of his very few appearances in Illingworth's wartime cartoons) – who had been pressing for a Second Front in the West for a long time – watching the flames of the burning city of Berlin. The quotation is from the last stanza of the poem 'Say Not the Struggle Nought Availeth' (1862) by Arthur Hugh Clough (1819-61). The full text reads:

And not by eastern windows only,
When daylight comes, comes in the light,
In front the sun climbs slow, how slowly,
But westward, look, the land is bright.

Illingworth had also alluded to this poem earlier in the war ('Eastward, look, the land is bright!' 7 July 1941) in a cartoon commenting on Stalin's 'scorched earth' defence of the USSR.

'But westward, look! the land is bright'
Daily Mail, 25 August 1943

Appointment With Fear
Daily Mail, 8 November 1943

Since 1940 the annual commemoration of the
Armistice that ended the First World War on
11 November 1918 had been banned in France
by the Vichy leader Marshal Pétain. However, on
Remembrance Day 1943 there was a large
demonstration in Grenoble, organised by the
French resistance, that led to 450 arrests.
Illingworth suggests that, like the Kaiser before
him, Hitler has a date with Death and is already
late for his appointment. (The film *Appointment
in Berlin* starring George Sanders was also
released in 1943.)

All Ready for the Operation
Daily Mail, 29 November 1943

On 28 November 1943 the main three Allied
leaders – Churchill, Roosevelt and Stalin – met
in the Iranian capital, Tehran, for a conference
to decide their strategy for the final conquest of
Germany and Japan. Illingworth shows the Big
Three as surgeons preparing to operate on Hitler
(bound and still conscious) while their aides –
(left to right) Foreign Secretary Anthony Eden,
Molotov and US Secretary of State Cordell Hull –
are depicted as theatre nurses.

Daily Mail, 2 December 1943

Three days before the Tehran Conference, Roosevelt, Churchill and China's leader Chiang Kai-Shek met in a hotel near the Pyramids in Cairo, Egypt, to discuss the next moves in the Pacific War against Japan. Though it was the seventh summit attended by the British and US leaders, it was the first one to include China. Illingworth's fat snake filled with 'Japan's Ill-Gotten Gains' has the face of Japan's military leader General Tojo. In the background Churchill, Chiang Kai-Shek (in the first of only two appearances by him in Illingworth's wartime cartoons) and Roosevelt prepare to slice it open.

The Last Act
Daily Mail, 22 December 1943

Illingworth uses a theatrical image in this cartoon. The 'last act' in the war will be the invasion of western Europe by Allied forces, the long-promised 'Second Front' which will squeeze Germany between it and the Soviet forces in the east, finally crushing the Nazis once and for all. This drawing shows the remnants of the German Wehrmacht, depicted as a single bloodied and exhausted foot soldier backing away from Soviet forces onto what he thinks is a safe, if somewhat tattered (note the patch) defensive fire-curtain, the Nazi's so-called Westwall. However, as can be seen, this is about to be raised to reveal massive British and US forces behind. The Christmas tree gives a festive pantomime feel to the cartoon and suggests that the audience might be about to shout 'Behind You...!'

1944

THE KEY EVENT OF 1944 was the opening of the long-awaited Second Front in the west of Europe. The massive Allied landings in Normandy on D-Day in June were followed by others in the south of France, and by the end of the year Paris and Brussels had been liberated from Nazi rule. Meanwhile, on the Eastern Front, Soviet forces finally broke out of the long siege of Leningrad and the Red Army launched massive attacks to sweep Axis troops from the Ukraine, Belorussia, Poland, Hungary and Romania. In the Pacific, the Battle of Leyte Gulf effectively destroyed what remained of the Japanese Fleet and despite suicide attacks by aircraft and ships and fanatical fighting by Japanese ground forces, it began to look like it was only a matter of time before the war finally ended in an Allied victory.

Spring Tide
Daily Mail, 13 March 1944

To symbolise the massive Soviet advances against the German Army Illingworth has Hitler as the eleventh-century King Canute attempting to hold back the sea in the form of a huge tidal wave (whose crest is Stalin) which has already engulfed Field Marshal Von Manstein (defeated in the Ukraine and later sacked by Hitler). Behind Hitler's throne cower figures representing the German public, Romania (which the Red Army would enter in April) and, already deserting him, Hungary.

Previous page: **Yes, Adolf, This Is It!** *Daily Mail*, 7 June 1944

One They Can't Lay
Daily Mail, 29 March 1944

The war in the east seemed to be going increasingly badly for the Nazis in the spring of 1944. As the Soviet Army invaded Bessarabia and threatened the borders of the Ukraine and Romania, non-stop Allied air-raids on Germany and occupied Europe took their toll on civilian morale.

In this cartoon the one ghost that the Nazis can't exorcise – the Spirit of German Defeat – kicks over the table on which Hitler and his generals examine their campaign plans for the Ukraine, Romania and Bessarabia. According to a report in the *Daily Mail* published on 19 July 1945 ('From Hitler's Private File – Himself, As Others Saw Him') a press-cutting of this drawing was one of a number by Illingworth found by Fusilier A.Hepton in the ruins of Hitler's Chancellery in Berlin after the war. With the symbols of Goebbels' propaganda ministry gummed to it, the cutting had been classified as item No.14947 and carefully filed (see also page 27).

Roman Holiday
Daily Mail, 29 May 1944

While the Red Army drove the Wehrmacht westwards, Allied forces in Italy – which had landed at Anzio, 32 miles south of Rome, in January – finally breached the Germans' Gustav Line at Cassino and advanced on the capital itself (which was liberated on 4 June by the US Fifth Army).

Illingworth has the British lion (representing the Eighth Army) chasing Field Marshal Kesselring (German commander-in-chief for the south of Italy and based in Rome), around the Colosseum which is full of joyful Italians waving Allied flags and banners labelled 'Viva Clark' and 'Viva Alexander' (the US and British commanders). ('Roman Holiday' is also an allusion to the death of a gladiator in Canto IV of Byron's *Childe Harold's Pilgrimage* [1818] 'Butchered to make a Roman holiday'.) This cartoon was published three months after Illingworth's elder brother, Lieutenant-Colonel Vivian Richard Illingworth OBE, died of leukaemia while on active duty in Naples on 2 February 1944.

**'...After the light is seen to go out, the machine dives
steeply and explodes on striking the ground'**
Daily Mail, 20 June 1944

In desperation against mounting odds, Hitler began to place his trust in a series of secret weapons that he believed could win the war by technological might. Amongst these were two kinds of long-range rocket-powered bomb, the V1 and the much larger V2. The first to appear on the scene was the V1, or doodlebug (the V stood for *Vergeltungswaffe* – reprisal weapon), which began to attack London in considerable numbers from northern France in mid-June 1944. Illingworth has Hitler as a V1 running out of fuel (German manpower) before it reaches its target.

127

'I have a comrade – I hope!'
Daily Mail, 24 July 1944

On 24 July 1944 an attempt was made by disaffected Nazi generals to assassinate Adolf Hitler
while he was at a conference in his 'Wolf's Lair' headquarters in Rastenburg, East Prussia.
Though the bomb left by Colonel Claus von Stauffenberg exploded and destroyed the building,
Hitler somehow survived and the conspirators were rounded up by Himmler. Illingworth shows
a Nazi general fleeing the burnt-out building to the safety of the Soviet front line. He is being
pursued by a hand-grenade as Himmler fires at him with a machine-gun and Hitler looks on.
'*Tovarich*' means 'comrade' in Russian (in this original Illingworth has spelt it *Tovarish*).

Daily Mail, 3 August 1944

By August 1944 things were looking brighter for the Allies. On 2 August Winston Churchill made a guarded, but for the first time quietly confident, speech in the House of Commons, saying that: 'I feel loth to raise false hopes, but I no longer feel bound to deny that victory may come perhaps soon.' Illingworth draws Churchill's face in the centre of a barometer with his cigar pointing to 'Set Fair' – indicating long-term good weather.

Too Late for Supper?
Daily Mail, 30 August 1944

As the Germans retreated, the former alliances they had forged with other countries
began to weaken and the Axis group of co-belligerents started to fall apart. Romania and
Bulgaria, which had both fought alongside the Nazis against the Allies, sued for a
separate peace in August 1944. Romania then declared war on Germany (25 August)
followed soon after by Bulgaria (7 September). Illingworth draws them as rats leaving
the sinking Nazi ship and climbing through the dining-room porthole of the Allies' boat.

Going Underground
Daily Mail, 6 October 1944

With the invasion of Germany itself by Allied forces in September the situation seemed to be increasingly desperate for the Wehrmacht leaders, many of whom had already been sacked by Hitler or were distrusted by their former Führer who was beginning to show signs of mental instability. Added to which, on 5 October 1944 Goebbels announced that food rations in Germany would be cut.

Illingworth envisages German generals stocking up with food, wine and other supplies as they move into a secret bunker hidden beneath a graveyard and await a future war in 1970 when their services will be required once more.

His Last Ally
Daily Mail, 20 November 1944

After the bomb plot against Hitler, Gestapo chief Heinrich Himmler began to wield
increasing power. In September 1944 he and Martin Bormann set up the *Volkssturm*
(or Home Guard) of young boys and old men in a last desperate attempt to hold off the
Allied forces now threatening Germany itself. Illingworth has drawn Himmler and 'Old
Man Winter' – the Nazis' last ally and armed with a hosepipe of freezing water –
making a last-ditch stand as regular German troops run away behind them.

1945

THOUGH 1945 WAS THE YEAR OF VICTORY for the Allies it was also perhaps the worst, in terms of human suffering, of all the years of the conflict. Firestorms caused by Allied bombing in Dresden in Germany and in Tokyo led to huge loss of life and as the concentration camps began to be liberated, the true scale of the Nazis' mass murder of Jews, gypsies and others became known. By the end of May Mussolini had been executed by Italian partisans, Hitler had committed suicide in Berlin and Germany had surrendered to the Allies unconditionally. However, the final horror was yet to come. On 6 and 9 August 1945 a new kind of weapon, based not on chemical high explosives but on the principle of nuclear fission, was detonated by US Air Force bombers above the Japanese cities of Hiroshima and Nagasaki. The loss of life was colossal, as was the power that the weapon's secret held for the future. The threat of further destruction by atomic bombs together with a simultaneous massive attack by the Soviet Union on Japanese forces in China, led to Japan's final surrender and the end of the Second World War.

Nemesis
Daily Mail, 29 January 1945

On 12 January 1945 Stalin began a major winter offensive with a mass attack on German positions in eastern Europe, taking Warsaw on the 17th and advancing 100 miles in a week. Soviet tanks (notably the mighty T-34) outnumbered German armour by five to one and by the 27th the Red Army was only 100 miles from Berlin (Soviet troops crossed the German border at the end of the month).

Illingworth has the spirits of Red Army soldiers, labelled Kiev, Stalingrad and Sebastapol – all scenes of bloody battles – crouched on the back of an enormous Soviet tank awaiting the chance to take their revenge as it thunders through the German countryside, crushing all in its path.

Previous Page: Daily Mail, 11 August 1945

The leader of the *Daily Mail* which appeared beside this cartoon was entitled 'Not Long Now' and began: 'The Third Reich is collapsing like a sandcastle surrounded by the incoming tide.' Illingworth uses another metaphor, depicting Hitler as a huge statue of a medieval knight in shining armour. Set on a cracked plinth amongst burning ruins, his sword is broken and his hand, raised in a Nazi salute, has crumbled away. The new Reich, which Hitler claimed would last for a 1000 years, was coming to an end.

THE REICH THAT WILL LAST 1000 YEARS

Daily Mail, 28 March 1945

To Last 1000 Years?
Daily Mail, 2 April 1945

The German retreat quickly became a rout as the Allies advanced across Europe and the Red Army closed in on Berlin. Time was running out for Hitler, for whom an honourable suicide seemed to be the only option left. In this cartoon a German general, keen to get on with the postwar situation, shows his impatience that Hitler is still alive. Meanwhile, in the background, other Nazi officers adjust the halo above the head of a statue of Hitler as a guardian angel and dust off its boots. (Note the face of Goebbels still hiding behind the 'Hitler Myth'.)

'Night passes...and the Evil Things depart'
Daily Mail, 8 May 1945

This wonderfully apocalyptic drawing, one of Illingworth's most powerful and dramatic creations of the war, was reproduced across six columns (nearly the entire width of the page) of the *Daily Mail* – almost twice the size of his usual drawings. The cartoon appeared on VE-Day (Victory in Europe Day) above a long article entitled 'After the Storm...' by Lord Vansittart, former chief diplomatic adviser to the British Government (1938-41). Recognisable amongst the bats, ghouls, ghostly horsemen, V1 flying bombs, Nazi generals and executioners fleeing the light of a new dawn are propaganda broadcaster Lord Haw-haw (with donkey head, bottom left), Propaganda Minister Goebbels (centre, still holding a microphone) and Heinrich Himmler. Hitler can be seen lying dead in the foreground. (In fact Goebbels himself was by this time also dead – he committed suicide on 1 May 1945 – but news of this had perhaps not reached Britain by this time.)

Stand-down
Daily Mail, 30 July 1945

This drawing marks the formal abolition or stand-down of the British Eighth Army which had fought so courageously in North Africa and Italy. Originally a much smaller group known as the Western Desert Force, it got its more famous name in the autumn of 1941. Here Churchill is seen shaking hands with an Eighth Army soldier, having written the final lines in a history book chronicling the German War, 1939 to 1945. The inkwell that holds his quill has written on it the words he uttered on 13 May 1940 in his first speech to the House of Commons after he became prime minister: 'I have nothing to offer but blood, toil, tears and sweat.'

Task Force
Daily Mail, 16 July 1945

There was a certain amount of poetic justice when the 'Big Three' Allied leaders –
Churchill, Truman (Roosevelt had died on 12 April) and Stalin – met at Sans Souci
Palace, in Potsdam near Berlin for a conference on the future of the postwar world.
For this had been the summer home of Frederick the Great, the first great Prussian
militarist, who had been greatly admired by Hitler.

'Isn't your way out hara-kiri?'
Daily Mail, 13 August 1945

Though the war in Europe was over – Prague was the last European capital to be liberated from
the Nazi yoke, on 9 May 1945 – the Pacific war against the Japanese continued with massive
aerial attacks on Tokyo and other cities by US bombers and fierce fighting on the island of
Okinawa and elsewhere. However, on 6 August 1945 the world's first atomic bomb was dropped
on Hiroshima, Japan's seventh largest city, with devastating results – nearly 80,000 died
instantly with thousands more dying of radiation sickness. Three days later another bomb was
unleashed on the shipbuilding port of Nagasaki. Shortly afterwards the Soviet Union declared
war on Japan.

In Illingworth's cartoon the ghosts of Mussolini and Hitler, the other two members of the
original Rome-Berlin-Tokyo Axis, stand before Japan's Emperor Hirohito as he considers the
Allies' final demand for unconditional surrender. His only honourable option seems to be
suicide by hara-kiri – ritual disembowelment using a ceremonial sword.

The Last Enemy
Daily Mail, 15 August 1945

The news of the Japanese surrender was officially
announced in Britain at midnight on 15 August 1945
– which would henceforth be known as VJ-Day
(Victory in Japan Day) – and on 2 September
Japanese Foreign Minister Shigemitsu headed the
delegation which signed the surrender document on
board the USS *Missouri* in Tokyo Bay. The Second
World War was finally over.

New Assignment
Daily Mail, 3 September 1945

With the war finally at an end, the immediate problem was that of world hunger, especially in those countries whose lands had been devastated during the conflict. This cartoon appeared next to a feature by John Langdon-Davies, the *Daily Mail*'s science editor, headed 'Acre after acre of food rots in the ground...while science holds key to plenty for all', recommending the use of atomic energy as a source of cheap power to regenerate the world.

Illingworth shows a scientist in the guise of the biblical David (note the sling) admiring his new invention and holding the head of Tojo as the defeated Goliath. Meanwhile, Humanity, in the shape of a young woman, points out that a new monster now needs his attention: World Starvation.

Index